Chris Packham's
Back Garden Nature Reserve

This book is for all those who have tasted tadpoles.

First published in 2001 by New Holland Publishers (UK) Ltd
London • Cape Town • Sydney • Auckland

2 4 6 8 10 9 7 5 3 1

86 Edgware Road, London W2 2EA, United Kingdom

80 McKenzie Street, Cape Town 8001, South Africa

Level 1/Unit 4, 14 Aquatic Drive, Frenchs Forest, NSW 2086, Australia

218 Lake Road, Northcote, Auckland, New Zealand

Photographic Acknowledgements
With the exception of those listed below, all the photographs in this book
were taken by David Cottridge:

CJ Wildbird Foods Ltd: p32; p138 • Colin Carver: p66 • E.A.Janes: p50 (t) • Gordon Langsbury: p34
• George McCarthy: p50 (br);p51 • Chris Packham: p8; p10; p11; p21 (t); p21 (b); p33 (tc); p53;
p55; p60; p90; p108 (br); p112; p113; p128; p129 (b); p130; p130 (t); p130 (bl); p131; p132;
p133 (t); 133 (b); 135 • Alan Petty : p49 • Richard Revels: p1; p12; p14; p63 (t); p63 (c); p63 (b);
p65; p67; p74 (tl); p74 (bl); p76 (t); p76 (bl); p78; p80; p82 (t); p82 (bl); p84; p85; p86; p87; p91
(tc); p92 (tr); p92 (c); p92 (bl); p93 (b); p96 (t); p96 (cr); p100; p104; p106; p107; p108 (tl);
p109; p111 (tr); p111 (tl); p111 (b); p116; p117 (c); p118; p119; p126; p127; p129 (b)
• David Tipling: p27 • The Wildlife Trusts: p7 • Alan Williams: p18; p21; p70; p74 (r); p94

t= top; b=bottom; c=centre; l=left; r=right

Artwork Acknowledgements
Artwork commissioned by Wildlife Art Ltd, www.wildlife-art.co.uk
Artists: Sandra Doyle and Cy Baker
Cover artwork: Sandra Doyle

Additional Artwork
Bird illustrations on the following pages by David Daly:
p16; p17; p28; p30; p31; p33; p38; p40; p41; p42; p43; p44;
p45; p46; p47; p48; p49; p136
Running headers on all pages by Greg Poole
Line artwork on pages 60 and 69 by Mike Unwin

ISBN 1 85974 520 2

Publishing Manager: Jo Hemmings
Project Editor: Mike Unwin
Copy Editor: Sylvia Sullivan
Designer: Roger Hammond
Cover Design: Alan Marshall
Diagrams: William Smuts
Index: Janet Dudley
Production: Joan Woodroffe

Reproduction by Modern Age Repro Co. Ltd, Hong Kong
Printed and bound in Malaysia by Times Offset (M) Sdn Bhd

CHRIS PACKHAM'S
BACK GARDEN
NATURE RESERVE

NEW HOLLAND

CONTENTS

PONDS

PLANTS

PHOTOGRAPHY

AFTER THOUGHTS

THE WILDLIFE TRUSTS

The Wildlife Trusts partnership is the UK's leading voluntary organisation working, since 1912, in all areas of nature conservation. We are fortunate to have the support of more than 325,000 members, including some famous household names.

This book's author Chris Packham – best known to readers perhaps as co-presenter of the BBC's *The Really Wild Show* – is President of the London Wildlife Trust and Vice-President of our junior club for children Wildlife Watch. And international naturalist and campaigner David Bellamy, who has provided the foreword, is President of The Wildlife Trusts and Wildlife Watch.

The Wildlife Trusts protect wildlife for the future by managing in excess of 2,300 nature reserves, ranging from woodlands and peat bogs, to heath lands, coastal habitats and wild flower meadows. We campaign tirelessly on behalf of wildlife, even in garden centres. With other leading environmental organisations, we continue the fight to persuade gardeners to boycott peat and limestone pavement – both vital habitats for many threatened species.

We also advise landowners, work to influence industry and government, and run thousands of events and projects for adults and children across the UK.

Our Wildlife Gardening initiative encourages people to take action for wildlife in their own back gardens. Readers may have picked up one of our wildlife gardening leaflets or may have seen The Wildlife Trusts Garden at BBC Gardeners' World Live, at the NEC. Visitors to our award-winning show garden included celebrity gardeners from the BBC's *Ground Force*, Alan Titchmarsh and Charlie Dimmock.

As traditional wildlife habitats in the countryside come under threat, as a result of modern farming techniques, development and water abstraction, gardens are becoming increasingly important. Gardens today are havens for many species of wildlife, providing food, shelter and breeding grounds as well as links to urban parks and other open spaces.

Many of the 46 Wildlife Trusts which together make up The Wildlife Trusts partnership, employ staff and volunteers to advise people on how best to encourage wildlife to their back yards. London Wildlife Trust even managed to persuade the Prime Minister Tony Blair to make space for a child-friendly wildlife pond in the garden at Number 10, Downing Street. It is amazing what a difference a few plants, logs or a pond can make to our wildlife, benefiting species as diverse as the Song Thrush, Painted Lady butterfly, Common Frog or Hedgehog.

Thank you for reading *Chris Packham's Back Garden Nature Reserve* and taking the time to discover how to create your very own wildlife haven.

The Wildlife Trusts is a registered charity (number 207238). For membership, and other details, please phone The Wildlife Trusts on 01636 677711.

FOREWORD
BY DAVID BELLAMY

In the UK we look after a staggering three million acres of garden, that's an area five times the size of greater London. Today every garden – however big or small – is a potential nature reserve. Over the past 50 years our countryside has suffered the destruction of much of its ancient woodlands, meadows and wetlands. We can't replace these losses, but in our gardens we can all do something for wildlife, and at the same time have some fun to boot!

This is why *Chris Packham's Back Garden Nature Reserve* is so important, helping people to create wildlife havens in their own back yard. I have known Chris Packham's work for a number of years now, not least because like me he supports The Wildlife Trusts and the junior club for children Wildlife Watch. Just like Chris, I appreciate the wonderful wildlife on my doorstep.

Many readers may wonder just why it is that planting alder trees and honeysuckle or creating a pond makes a difference. These days gardens form a patchwork of wildlife habitats, linking urban green spaces with nature reserves and the wider countryside and have become increasingly important for many species. Red squirrels, for example, recently hit the headlines after finding refuge – alongside top executives, successful footballers and pop stars – in some of the very smartest addresses in Cheshire. But it is not just large gardens in up-market addresses that are home to wildlife. Even inner city window boxes can provide food and shelter for a range of birds and insects. Making the UK's 15 million gardens wildlife-friendly will help plants and animals and will ensure that wildlife is there for future generations of people to know and experience.

Wildlife gardening breathes life into anyone's garden, whether in the town or country. A small pond, a marvellous meadow bed and a log pile – even a hedgerow – are not so difficult to create. Remember wildlife just needs four things from your garden – food, water, shelter and places to breed. *Chris Packham's Back Garden Nature Reserve* spells out the importance of creating places that allow wildlife to thrive alongside people and, shows how, with a little tolerance and resourcefulness, we can all be truly 'green'-fingered in our gardens.

I hope you will enjoy this book as much as you enjoy your garden, packed with the sight, sounds, smells, action and beauty of wildlife.

Happy wildlife gardening!

David Bellamy: President, The Wildlife Trusts and Wildlife Watch

INTRODUCTION

It's there, in the dark, in the shadows, waiting. It's watching. It's stalking.

A dry rustle as it shifts among the grass, still hidden, and while we strain to see it, I know it can see us. It's a predator; its eyes are keener than ours, its senses sharper, its jaws sharper still. Again it moves in the deep shade; I remain frozen, suffocating on a long held breath, conscious that just a blink might betray us. I wonder what it would be like to be seized, shaken and crushed, to have it standing over me, its cold and merciless menace staring me in the face. I wonder what I'll think and feel, me the big clever human, me who can drive cars, fire guns, fly in aircraft and write books – me not so clever when I'm just another item of prey.

A bead of sweat runs from my brow into my eye. My vision blurs and, as if it has sensed my instant weakness, now it launches into attack. It moves quickly, twice I see the foliage shiver and feel my body surge as it storms towards me, superior, confident, strong, a natural-born killer with that instinct flaming in its screaming eyes.

"Tea-time", shouts my girlfriend from the balcony as the Violet Ground beetle scuttles past my wrist and I kneel up in the rank grass that dominates our garden. Megan, aged five, and I trudge up the sunny path to the house to tell mummy how we've just cheated death. We had been crawling around pretending we were Woodlice, taking a closer look at life in our little bit of the real world.

In the kitchen there's a cup of Earl Grey, a cup of orange squash, some biscuits and a programme about tigers on TV. The tea is great, but the TV fails to command our attention. The tigers are in India, not in Netley near Southampton, and we've just had a real encounter with a super predator. We smelled him and felt him. He was un-edited, he lives in our garden, he's part of our community, he's relevant to us. Would you enjoy a cup of Earl Grey if it was on TV?!

Opposite: Simple and stunning. A male Brimstone butterfly competes for brilliance with Knapweed and Ragwort. It's not rare, it's not exotic and with any luck this palette might be on your patch.

Left: At home in our personal reserve. There's lots of work to do yet, but successfully sharing our space with other animals is the goal.

Our society is obsessed with celebrity: Posh and Becks, glamorous gardeners, Manchester United and Coronation Street. And worse, conservation and natural history have fallen under a similar spell. Tigers, gorillas, sharks and the pandas that might mate in San Diego Zoo. Sometimes it's difficult to assess which has least relevance; maybe the pandas could actually sing, perhaps the gorillas wouldn't be sent off at the most crucial moments (I suspect the sharks certainly would!). But seriously, aren't we in danger of ignoring the most exciting species of all – those which we can touch, smell and enjoy every day in our own backyard? Those animals which quite literally help shape the community in which we live, who make our gardens grow or not. And if something is rare, who is better placed to conserve it than the people who live with it? Who is better equipped to effect an immediate and positive influence and, this is the big one, enjoy the fruits of their endeavours first hand? I'm not saying that it isn't worth putting a pound in the pot to save tigers, just that you'll be relying on an Indian, Nepali, Siberian or Sumatran to actually do the work, and if they do, they'll be the ones watching the tiger. Whereas, if you put a pond in your patch you'll get to see the dragonfly that comes with just as much ferocity to prey upon any smaller species. And if that scale bothers you then lie down and pretend to be a Woodlouse. If it does the trick for Megan and myself, then I'm sure it will for you too!

Being an Animal

Imagining that you are invertebrate prey is a good first step in re-assessing yourself in the natural community – just because you know about arithmetic, art, advertising or angina doesn't mean you're not an animal. For all of our consciousness, intellect, technology and religion we are still living, breathing, eating, defecating and reproducing animals. If we had better sense we would ensure that we

remained in harmony with the communities of other organisms around us. Because that sense has deserted us, the environment, our environment, is in the state it is today. I blame it on the way we pretend that we are not animals any more, that we are above playing by nature's rules. Well, if you'll forgive the vulgar honesty, ask some cod fishermen if they are above the rules of nature, ask the flooded refugees in Mozambique or the beef farmers who fed sheep to cows or all the increasing number of drought victims all over the world. If you abuse the system too much it breaks. Mending it may still be possible but only if we all make an effort and remember that we're not repairing it just for all the other species of animals but for our own species of animal too.

Ancient Trees

A simple problem that conservationists continually face is that people only seem able to measure natural events in terms of the human life-span. This is an obvious flaw.

Some readers may live near ancient Yew trees. In recent years a Yew tree campaign initiated by Alan Meredith has led to the documentation of these trees and in many cases steps to aid their preservation. Trees are registered, measured and certificates issued. The Conservation Foundation has maps and details if you're interested. Ageing the trees is difficult owing to their growth pattern, naturally hollow, which means counting annual growth rings is impossible. Besides, the girth of one 2.1 m midget was sectioned after

Above: *Urban survivor. An adder sneaks down some discarded tyres, potent and perfectly patterned. Not an ideal garden guest for many, but a beautiful and valuable addition to any local community.*

the 1987 storm and yielded more than three hundred rings. The growth of Yews is slow; some measure more than 16 m in girth and although it was thought that fifteen hundred years was a realistic estimate (often confirmed by documented historical reference) it is now believed that these trees may live between five and eight thousand years. Sit under one and think about this.

Typically in churchyards, these sacred trees were alive before your gods were born. Before language, before writing, before our species was civilized in any way. These totems of life on Earth defy our petty ideas and arrogance. They stand sentinels to a far greater force and should serve to remind us that, not only our individual existence, but that of our species is a mere spark in the greater line of life past, present and future. We can't imagine eight thousand years because we live for only eighty.

We are small. Small potatoes. What we do is small. Of course, we've done so much in so little time but we've also had an equally rapid and disastrous effect on ourselves and our future which isn't quite so clever. We've run away with ourselves and forgotten the Yew, standing there slowly straining our corpses from the hallowed soil and involving us in its long, long life. Sit for a while beneath its scented boughs and breathe in the age, pick up a twig and know that the world's oldest wooden artefact is a spear made 150,000 years ago and that a similar item was found embedded in the rib cage of a fossilized straight-tusked Mastodon. Think! that tree whispering above you may have been planted by a Neolithic human on a burial ground, that it certainly provided a spiritual focus for Celtic peoples for whom it epitomized a belief in immortality. Gaze out at something redolent of the twenty-first century, a new car, a mobile phone, a skyscraper or jet aircraft and ask yourself if we do justice to that simplicity or have we all forgotten, got lost in big ideas.

Life without a consciousness of nature and its balance will prove to be a gimmick, a fad, a boom bubble that will burst and leave us stranded. We smile, we agonize, we cry today, ours is this present. But yesterday's Yew has tomorrow too and all the things that creep amongst it will crawl and the same smell will seep from its pores and the leaves whisper the same songs in the wind. As you creep from its shade into the sunshine of century twenty-one feel a little more real, a little more animal, a little more aware of those organisms we all but ignore as we speed along. After all, you know what they say about he who laughs last.

Your Resources

But then what's all this sobering reality got to do with wildlife gardening? Well, contrary to some leanings and the title, this is not a book about wildlife gardening in the traditional, dig it, plant it and wait and see mode. It is a book designed to promote the practice of co-existing harmoniously with other species of animal in the places where we live, work and play. It's about modifying your resources, however modest or magnificent, to increase their value to other species of animal and not just the cuddly and glamorous ones either. For instance, you won't see the word 'pest' outside of inverted commas because I do not recognize the term in that context. I see competitors and rivals for a resource that we desire, I see champions and cannot blame other life for trying and succeeding, certainly not in the face of human arrogance. Just like the classroom, on the factory floor, or in the office – in your garden or your community it takes all sorts and, let's face it, if you suddenly open a fully stocked supermarket specializing in the finest ripe vegetable materials you've got to expect a few shoppers!

Natural Chaos

Besides which, the concept of gardening is ecologically 'dodgy' anyway. I haven't checked my dictionary but gardening by definition seems to me to be the enforcement of artificial order over nature's organisation.

Nature can be chaotic, untidy, even ugly through its random complexity. Think of a tree that has twisted under the continual attrition of the wind, that is tilted in an untoward manner. Perhaps a couple of branches have died and it thus appears unbalanced, one-sided and it doesn't complement any grand design for a picturesque environment. In fact, it's a blight upon it. It's a hideous misshapen freak and it's making your garden look bad, offending your sense of symmetry, and even your ideal of the term 'tree'. You want to cut it down, to remove this wart, to be neat and to be tidy.

But the tree is an aged native, a willow, a birch, even an old oak. Within its tatty canopy resides a whole community unconcerned by your alien ideas of order. For them the tree is an essential resource, a little island where they live. That scar on the trunk is not the wound you think it is. That cavity is home to myriad creatures, doing a job, evolving, feeding, surviving alongside you without doing you any harm. They share your time and place in the great grand scheme of things, quite unconcerned by tidiness. And theirs is an organization too complex for us to begin to understand, a functional, dynamic perfection which no gardener

Above: Submerged in a silvery jacket of air, the magnificent Raft spider is a pond predator par excellence. A photograph taken in my garden and a vee tank success. (See pages 134–135 for technique).

could ever aspire too. So bring a more open mind to nature's chaos. Shape it with sensitivity, mould it with consideration, admit its honesty and enjoy its humour. Control is always the alter ego of tolerance in the garden. Relax, let go, get absorbed, share your space. Look in the mirror – you're not symmetrical or perfect either!

But please don't think that I'm anti garden or anti gardening. There are nearly three million acres of gardens in Britain and, paradoxically, as our suburban countryside is systematically ravaged to satisfy our desire to own homes, the accompanying gardens can often be richer than the habitats they are laid over. One important measure of value from the conservationist perspective is biodiversity, and not many habitats can vie with our gardens on this account. In a normal British suburban garden there can be as many as 250 different species of plant. This remarkable figure is far higher than could be recorded anywhere in our countryside

and although more than half are probably non-native species, this value as a food source is unrivalled. In fact at the height of summer the blazing beds and borders of a British garden produce a greater array of scents and nectar than you could find in any tropical paradise. Not surprisingly, traditional gardens are havens for insects.

A Closer Look

In the late 1970s an entomologist took a closer look at his garden in the suburbs of Leicester. Quite amazingly he recorded eight of the nineteen species of British bumblebee, eighty-three of the 250 hoverfly and 529 of the two thousand species of Ichnuemon family of parasitic wasp. In this last group he found several species unrecorded in Britain and two tiny chaps previously unknown to science! Don't tell me you need to go to the heart of New Guinea to discover a new species – you may just need to go outside!

In the same garden Dennis Owen found twenty-one of the sixty British species of butterfly. Over ninety-five per cent of his fluttering visitors belonged to just six species: Large White, Small White, Green-veined White, Red Admiral, Small Tortoiseshell and Peacock, but other gems included the White-letter Hairstreak, Small Blue, Painted Lady and Silver-washed Fritillary. His garden was only 4 km from the city centre yet his totals bettered all those recorded on local nature reserves. Indeed, in his relatively tiny garden, he recorded eighty-four per cent of the butterfly species ever recorded in the nine hundred square kilometres of the British Midlands surrounding his home. Pretty impressive, even though he was unhappy about the absence of Holly-Blue and Clouded Yellow butterflies! But that was the 1970s, some thirty years ago, and sadly since then there have been dramatic declines in some species that we took for granted or even considered common.

As far as I can ascertain, from the middle ages through to the beginning of the nineteenth century, gangs of resourceful boys would prowl the lanes in search of those favoured ivy-clad walls where House Sparrows roosted *en masse* each autumn and winter. Caught easily in large soft

Right: *Newts, one of many childhood favourites, but hardly the most enthralling creatures outside the breeding season. They are essential but not exciting pond dwellers.*

nets and by the tens or hundreds, the birds were a welcome addition to any peasant's pot and the practice was encouraged as farmers resented the twittering competition for their grain stock. I can only remember one such roost as a boy, with maybe fifty to a hundred birds, perhaps enough for one bony meal and now, well I'm glad there are no peasants relying on such a harvest to stave off starvation because House Sparrows, like Skylarks, Partridges and even Starlings, are on the way out. In the last thirty years their population has declined by no less than fifty-eight per cent.

It's not currently popular to point the finger frankly and precisely, indeed only the most confrontational conservationist will indulge, but the culprits here are not those scruffy lads and their nets. In no uncertain terms those that set and maintain our farming policies have the blood of our bird life on their hands. Too intensive, over too great an area for too long, and lo and behold the finely tuned, beautiful balance of nature has been broken. Herbicides, pesticides, phosphates, nitrates and monocultures. Ponds filled, hedgerows grubbed, woodlands felled, and worst of all everything kept so horribly, so unnaturally tidy.

Farming and Policy

Now of course the farmers aren't the bad guys. A great many farmers like and enjoy wildlife as much as you or I, and many have done far more to help it than we'll ever manage, but the overall management practice is flawed, outdated and in desperate need of reform. Surely we all perceive wine lakes and butter mountains as vile embarrassments, especially when they're paid for in Skylarks and Yellowhammers. But how about the farmer, how does he feel tending the crop he knows is unwanted even before it is planted? Some bemoan his grants and subsidies and the artificial pricing of his produce or harvest, a system alien in most other markets. But what if those subsidies were used to farm countryside instead, to replant hedgerows, to re-dig ponds, who better to do it than those who know how to grow, who know their land – the farmers? This beleaguered industry needs our support and when they get it, it works. The crofting community of the north-west of Scotland have pretty much single-handedly saved the Corncrake from extinction in Britain. The RSPB devised the method, the EC offered some financial incentives, but it was the farmers who actually did the job. So who or what is the problem? The problem is the Common Agricultural Policy, a poorly devised and outdated strategy that is killing our countryside and all the wildlife that lives in it faster than anything else. And guess what, it is managed in Europe and any revision takes place in the face of active opposition from the vociferous French and Spanish farming fraternities – not collectives known for their keen conservation of songbirds!

So the immediate prognosis is not great – too many suits, too few ecologists, too many greedy lobbyists and too few quick and effective decisions. If only they'd listened to Skylarks from their school playgrounds, if only they'd jumped over the fence and searched through the dusty grass for their nests and knelt in awe above those little grassy cups filled with smudged brown eggs, each one a trill, a chorus, a crescendo in waiting. Then perhaps they'd act a little more positively and promptly. But then history reliably shows that we cannot rely upon politicians to enact what we want, even if we vote for them.

Above: *A resplendent cock pheasant. A paradox, in that because people shoot them, they are surviving. People listen to Skylarks but that's not enough. Our countryside is in a mess so take control.*

Do Something

So if we care, here are our options: moan about it; expect people who don't care to fix it; wait for someone else to motivate them and save the world: or help, do something ourselves. To me the last option seems the best. A little practical, direct action can be satisfying and effective. If you have a garden, in fact if you own anything from a window box to a country estate, then within reason you can manage it. You won't be encouraged to plough it or be paid to poison or pollute it or to discourage everything living from visiting it. And collectively with all of our gardens and all of our resources the potential is staggering. You can help buck the trend and however small your patch is it will make a difference. Even if you can't create a neighbourhood national park or a miniature Minsmere you can offer some small or struggling species a little salvation. The aim of this book is to suggest a few methods, offer a few tips and ignite your enthusiasm and ingenuity. You are the wardens of our 'Back Garden Nature Reserves', arm yourself with information, summon a little energy, come up with a few ideas and enjoy the rewards first hand, not on TV.

In the text that follows I have tried to be pragmatic. I like things that work – I'm not so keen on fantasy. Often though, different practices vary in their effectiveness, so for all of my advice it is down to you to adapt my suggestions to fit your schemes or spaces. I must also fully confess that I am not a gardener by any means, I am an ecologist and a lover of life, of all life. I am also impatient and not alone in this failing, so, many of the ideas proffered are designed for immediate or rapid results. We live dangerously fast lives; few of us have one garden per lifetime so my plans have been drawn to fit feasible reward schedules, most in five years or less. Of course longer term schemes are included and essential but this is not a book full of ideas you'll need to age to enjoy. If you do, then it's a bonus.

I'm sure you'll find a few of my essays a little radical, my love of wasps and tolerance of flies and rats even a little bizarre, but while I tease with extremist humour I have a genuine foundation of intent here and it is one based upon respect. If just one family leaves a wasp nest to fulfil its cycle in their loft, if one wife or husband decides not to spray those flies but to cover their food instead, if one more little boy sneaks out to feed his rats then my trouble would have been worthwhile. I don't expect fan clubs to spring up, I just hope a few folks will think twice.

So let's get down to planning your back garden nature reserve. Every garden is unique, so what you do and where will be peculiar to you. But one fundamental technique that will prove invaluable is assessing what you can offer any species you wish to attract. The best way to progress is to learn a little about its life, its ecology, its requirements and then devise an offer it will not refuse. The first three sections are designed to illustrate this, a mammal (Hedgehog), a bird (Great Tit) and an insect (Small Tortoiseshell butterfly), are defined as a set of sample species. Through analysis of their known requirements we can easily make that offer...

Hedgehogs
FLATTENED, HUNGRY AND HOMELESS

We like Hedgehogs. We like the way they snuffle and bumble about like over-clad elderlies at a church bazaar. We like their apparently cuddly but very prickly coats and their neat little black noses flexing about, sniffing and snorting loudly. Their young are undeniably cute and they eat slugs, which, being a lot less popular in the zoological top one hundred, makes them another of the gardeners 'friends'. So why do we squash so many on our roads? Why have gardeners betrayed them by using nasty molluscicides that starve them out or poison them? Like so many animals we have grown up with and taken for granted, Hedgehogs now need our help.

Above and left: *Happy, healthy hogs are a charming addition to any garden's fauna and very easy to attract and satisfy. Sit outside late into the evening and investigate suspicious snufflings stealthily to see if you've got spikey visitors.*

Profile

Hedgehogs are insectivores and thus closely related to moles and shrews with which they share similarities in the dental department – sharp pointed teeth. Spines, each measuring up to 2.2 cm, entirely replace hairs on the back and are moulted irregularly, each lasting at least eighteen months. These offer superb protection to the adults, which can roll into a ball to completely shield all extremities and can erect and relax the spines at will. Sometimes Hedgehogs weigh over a kilogram but their weight varies dramatically as they lose as much as thirty per cent each winter during hibernation, which usually begins in October and ends at the beginning of April. Hedgehogs can slow their heartbeats from one hundred and ninety to twenty beats a minute and chill down to four degrees Centigrade.

Hedgehogs can be found all over Britain and Ireland, and on many islands where they have been introduced. Their favoured habitat is rank grassland adjacent to woodland or hedgerows through meadowland, but they can also be found anywhere where there is enough cover for nesting and adequate food. Beetles, caterpillars, centipedes, spiders, the occasional bird's egg or chick, and earthworms supplement their slug favouring menu. They are said to eat snakes but are not resistant to Adder's venom and would have to rely on their spines for protection from its fangs. If I were a Hedgehog I'd stick to slugs!

Normally five young are born into a specially made nest in mid-summer. They leave after three weeks and after a further three weeks of weaning go their own way. For a short while they may be vulnerable to foxes and badgers but typically they have no more problems other than your Michelins, Pirellis or Dunlops.

You and Hedgehogs

Okay, you didn't break or swerve and you're feeling guilty, what can you do to ease your guilt and help the local hogs? Basically all the information you need to get started is contained in the profile above. By analysing their ecological requirements you can easily deduce how you can adapt your garden to become Hedgehog compatible.

Do you have Hedgehogs in your garden? Well, they are nocturnal so you could easily miss them unless you look and listen for their loud snuffling and sniffing between April and October. Alternatively check for footprints or droppings (black, full of insects, 1 cm diameter, up to 5 cm long and fairly firm) or, sadly, check your gutter for corpses.

If they do visit, then provide them with food and water to guarantee regular sightings. Place the food in semi-lit areas and they'll soon get used to the light. Bread and milk was the staple suggestion for these animals but it probably did for as many as the A1 and M5 ever has. Do not feed these animals cows' milk – it is too rich. Dog and cat food, dusted occasionally with a vitamin powder, is ideal, or you could try a commercial Hedgehog food mix. These feature dried meat, insects, berries and nuts, and need to be accompanied by plenty of fresh water because of their dried nature.

Making Hogs at Home

Okay, now Hedgehogs are visiting regularly, what about offering them a permanent home? All you need is a well drained and quiet corner to build yourself a hibernaculum. At its most basic all that's required is a metre square 'log camp', about 30-40 cm high, packed with dry grass, hay and leaves and covered with a stout plastic tent. This should be further buried beneath more logs and leaves to secure and hide the roof and also provide adequate insulation. A plywood box with a clear ventilation hole and waterproof roof, again filled with dry bedding, is a step up the housing ladder and will obviously last longer, as might either the wooden or plastic commercially available Hedgehog nest boxes. These cost about twenty-five pounds but will require just as much care in siting to become attractive to the homeless hog.

Left : Don't do this with a wild hedgehog. It will ball-up, spike you or even give you a non-life-threatening but annoying bite. Even a tame creature like this one can be a handful – a little spine grenade.

Artificial feeding and housing are immediate solutions and will generally work, but a more constructive and proper course of conservation is habitat management. Don't worry, you won't be needing a tractor, calling in contractors or breaking your back with hard work. In fact the reverse in this instance – it's less work that's required. Fence off a strip of garden 1.5 m wide by as long as you can, say a minimum of 3 m, and clear it of all herbage. Go for a walk in the local countryside and fill a bag with seed heads from big coarse non-lawn grasses and scatter these on your fallow field. Water and nourish. Plant a couple of brambles which will eventually consolidate the emergent tangle and restrict access to nosey foxes and cats. Every few years hack half of it back in summer and allow it to recover. This will create a natural refuge for Hedgehogs and of course a diversity of other life and if there are any complaints from 'er or 'im indoors promise them a blackberry pie. One last word – fleas. Hedgehogs can be heavily infested with fleas, up to five hundred on one animal. The species concerned is *Archaeopsylla erinacei* and it is entirely specific to the Hedgehog. That's to say it will definitely not cross infect your dog, cat, hamster or child. You are not at risk from Hedgehog parasites but should not handle wild hogs through the risk of biting, which is fairly fierce, and the resultant risk of other infections.

Above and right: Beware bonfires. Please don't unintentionally barbecue nesting or hibernating hogs – check your leaf or log piles, and rake them over before you build your bonfire.

15

GREAT TITS

BIG, BRASH, BOLD AND BOLSHY!

The day had begun grey, a pool of smoke the size of England shading half of Sumatra. Now it was raining wet ash and the ground was going grey too. The temperature had fallen and an apocalypse was in progress. As we slid across sludge through the tea plantations and up to the forest edge my disappointment was impossible to hide. This should be paradise, a tropical rain forest with tigers, tapirs, and a myriad other sparkling species. Instead we were entering hell. I waited an hour and then set off to see some birds. It was silent, just the whisper of drizzle on a million leaves. Then, right beside me, I heard a startling call 'teacherr-teacherr'. Startling not because of its volume but because of its familiarity. I looked and yes, here in the distant hell of burning Sumatra, the first bird I saw was a Great Tit, and I liked that! What a species, what a success, what a survivor! I like Great Tits, they're great!

Profile

The Great Tit is, as you might expect, the largest of the seven British tits and clearly the most strikingly marked with its bold black, white and chrome yellow plumage. At the bird feeder it is also the most dominant and demonstrative, regularly striking strange poses to its cons-specific co-feeders! Males are markedly brighter than females whereas juveniles are much duller, almost sooty looking.

No other British birds have such a broad repertoire of notes and calls. If you're in the garden and you hear an unfamiliar bird, I bet you a pound it's a Great Tit. 'Chink', 'Tink', 'Tsee', 'Pee' and 'Cha-Cha-Cha' are

Right: What a pair! Their sulphur yellow breasts and contrasting black stripes and caps make the species a striking little spectacle.

Left: Striking a pose. Watch a group of Great Tits on a bird feeder and you're sure to spot some curious antics, but what do they mean?

typical utterances, but there are thousands more where they come from.

Great Tits are one of Britain's commonest birds and in their favoured native habitat of mature broad-leaved woodland will occur at densities of up to a pair per two acres (0.8 hectares). In groups of gardens with well stocked feeders the densities can be even higher. Because they are heavier and less agile than the remainder of their family they forage lower down on the trunks and even on the ground. The nesting site is a hole and chamber of some kind which is filled with a mound of moss and the cup lined with hair or fur – not feathers like the other tit species. Five to fifteen, normally eight or nine, pale and red spotted eggs are laid in late April, incubated solely by the female whilst the male feeds her, for about fourteen days. The young fledge after nearly three weeks and are independent in less than a month. Like other tits this species feeds primarily on insects in summer and seeds in winter. Of course the Great Tit's larger size means that it can handle larger types of either food. Beetles, bees (stings are removed), butterflies, moths and bugs all feature but there is even a record of a particularly predatory Great Tit killing a Goldcrest and flying off 'hawk-like' with its victim clasped in its feet. In winter its fluctuating vegetarian favourites are beechmast and hazelnuts, and of course peanuts, all of which they will cache for future use. By feeding marked food, scientists have found that Great Tits' memories are not as great as their name and lots of hidden fruits get to enjoy germination.

Above: *Fanned tail, cocked head and flattened cap, this bird is saying something to someone!*

Right: *Groups of the dusky and generally duller juveniles may swamp your feeders after fledging in summer. Be sure to offer plenty of water too.*

You and Great Tits

The best thing about biology is that it all makes sense. It has to or else it wouldn't happen. Nature's intolerance of waste is unrelenting. I think it's easier to be a biologist than any other scientist; all you have to do is watch, listen and think of questions, which you then answer by further observation. If you want to get to grips with Great Tits you simply have to offer them alternatives. It's easy to see whether you have Great Tits. If you're more than two hundred metres from any substantial greenery, bushes or maturing trees the signs won't be good as these birds normally need that sort of cover. Try putting out a feeder for a few weeks and if they appear you won't fail to scc them. If they're around offer them the right foods; serve peanuts in

a safely sited feeder or loose on a table in the winter and either ensure your garden is rich in insects throughout the summer, or purchase live foods to supplement the natural supply. Because they are bolder and less bashful than their cousins, it's easier to get close to Great Tits. They'll be the first onto any window-placed feeders and can even be trained to pinch peanuts from your hand – a neat, but naughty trick!

Nesting

Now Great Tits have a thing about nest boxes. They'll actually move out of any natural sites in favour of sound and sensibly sited artificial boxes. They're the easiest of all of our birds to encourage to rear a family in proximity to us. The reason that this doesn't happen all over suburbia is simply down to vital statistics – the diameter of the entrance hole and the volume of the chamber. Most of the better boxes you can buy at garden centres or DIY stores are designed for Blue Tits, a species often reticent to take up these proffered residences. Twenty-five millimetres will allow Blue, Coal and even Marsh Tits into the box, but you need a full 32 mm diameter hole for Great Tits – any smaller and the squeeze is simply too much. Also they like more room inside to fill with a minor mountain of moss. The best option is to build your own bigger boxes. Longer term options include planting Beech, Hawthorn and Holly, which will soon bush out and offer cover near your feeder as this added security will guarantee a larger and happier flock of foragers. Trees such as Birch, which support a healthy crop of caterpillars in summer and a nutritious mass of buds in late winter and spring, are also favourites with all the tit species.

SMALL TORTOISESHELLS

Beneath a gossamer tent in an emerald glow filtering through the serrated panes of the high canopy the larval army is marching. Prickly black and minutely jewelled with white and broken yellow it wobbles and weaves through the forest of glistening spines that jut from each vein and stalk. But the spines are no defence for the marauders. If no path can be picked through stickles they are chomped away, disappearing quickly at the mercy of mechanical jaws into the jet black capsules. High above, spectrums flutter on flashing wings, searching areas to lay a new horde in waiting. It's a Nettle bed in May or June; it could be anywhere from Europe to Japan or in any part of Britain. The species is so familiar that it is ignored, a sad fate for such a successful star of so many continents. That spiney army will metamorphose into Small Tortoiseshell butterflies and where would Versace or Hermes or Montana be without them? If you measure glamour as glitz, then your garden ought to be a fashionable haven for these dandies.

Profile

Parks and gardens, wastelands, woodlands, in fact anywhere there are nectar-bearing flowers within the vicinity of Nettles, the only larval food plant, are the habitats of Small Tortoiseshell butterflies. There are two broods a year: one hatches in August, hibernates over winter, emerges in March, mates and lays the second brood, which is on the wing in late May or June. The tiny eggs are pale green and laid in a large batch on the underside of a Nettle leaf. The caterpillars are dark grey to begin with, then blacker. They live in communal webs until they are half grown and then forage singly or in twos and threes in the protection of folded or curled leaves. The pupae are dull brown, washed with a golden sheen and hang head down from a plant stem, usually not that of the food plant. As adult butterflies they have mainly avian predators. I've seen Great Tits, Spotted Flycatchers, Robins and House Sparrows all flying off with Tortoiseshells and once watched Hornets hammering both these, and their larger relatives Red Admirals, in an orchard. The brutal Hornets knock the butterflies to the ground and then pin them down. Dramatic death follows; first the head is nipped off and then the wings, the rest is chewed into a bolus of indiscernible flesh and carried off to the nest. If any meat remains the ever-hungry Hornet will return and carry this off as well. Nothing is wasted and the whole exercise is cruel but rather neat.

As larvae the Small Tortoiseshell is plagued with predators, not least through the specific attentions of parasitic Ichneumonid wasps, which lay their eggs directly onto the caterpillars' skin. When they hatch they do so inwards, straight into the living meat! The young wasp is programmed to avoid eating the vital organs so that the caterpillar lives on, sometimes even successfully pupating before the wasp grub does so itself and of course it emerges first, killing the butterfly in the process. Other species of parasite use long ovipositors to lay their eggs inside the larvae whereas others lay them onto the food plant ready to be eaten by the hungry caterpillars. Some are even laid into the butterflies' eggs and don't emerge until the pupal stage. These tiny parasites often appear insignificant but have life histories which make the storylines of our favourite soaps look dull. Spiders, particularly common Crab Spiders, are also a menace to these butterflies, as are dragonflies and robberflies.

You and Small Tortoiseshells

Butterflies have even simpler requirements than birds and mammals. Just about all you have to do is feed them. Almost unbelievably I recently found, in an otherwise normally stocked garden centre, a device purporting to be a 'butterfly feeder'. The plastic box was described as a valuable addition to any garden and appeared to contain a liquid nectar substitute, which apparently serves to attract these 'important pollinators'. It comes in red and yellow versions and cost £7.95. Are they mad? Those that made it, those who sell it and those who buy it? I mean artificial flowers are okay for doctors' waiting rooms, your crazy aunt's bathroom, and uninspiring restaurant tables, but the idea of replacing a real flower with a red plastic tub full of sugar water to feed a butterfly is frankly not on. Let's stick to real plants to promote your garden, not only to Tortoiseshells but also a host of other species.

Adult butterflies require fuel not food. They are merely mobile mating machines so they need a high energy activator and that means nectar. Some species of plant produce more nectar than others and replenish it more

The silken web provides a modicum of protection from larger predators but not the insidious attention of parasitic wasps.

Freshly hatched larvae gather in clots beneath the web where they feed furiously on the succulent leaf tips.

Gravid females search the nettle bed for areas free of caterpillars that could compete with her potential brood.

Female Tortoiseshell egg laying onto soft fresh and succulent shoot, an ideal meal for her brood.

More mature larvae forage singly, having left the security of the web and rely on wriggling and dropping from the leaf to escape larger predators.

The cryptic chrysalis hangs in the shade for 2-3 weeks before the adult emerges.

quickly – these are our target species. Because none of them flower throughout the period that the adult insects are on the wing it is necessary to 'organise' a sequence of successive bouquets to deliver the goods. See box on the right for the top ten.

All of these plants grow well in restricted space, in typical garden soils and are low maintenance easy-care species. The Buddleia is the best all rounder but soon gets straggly and unkempt, and thus needs a moderate cut back each winter. The Michaelmas Daisy and Ice Plants generally prove to be magnets for Tortoiseshells, Red Admirals, Commas and Peacocks in the autumn when all the nectar has drained away from the rest of the garden.

Many butterflies are species specific when it comes to their larval food plant and Small Tortoiseshells are no exception – it's Stinging Nettles (*Urtica dioica*) or bust. I know Nettles are unpopular with the kids because they sting a bit, but you'll need no more than a couple of square metres to get started. Rake a patch of clear soils, put heaps of nitrogen based fertiliser on it, scatter a fair whack of nettle seeds and rake in either in the autumn or

NECTARFUL PLANTS FOR YOUR BORDERS

Spring flowering	Aubrieta (*A. deltoidea*)
	Yellow Alyssum (*A. saxatile*)
	Honesty (*Lunaria* sp)
	Sweet Rocket (*Hesperis matronalis*)
Summer flowering	Valerian (*Centranthus* sp)
	Lavender (*Lavandula* sp)
Summer/Autumn flowering	Buddleia (*Buddleia* sp)
	Tobacco Plant (*Nicotiana alata*)
Autumn flowering	Ice Plant (*Sedum spectabile*)
	Michaelmas Daisy (*Aster novae velgii*)

spring. The species is a fierce competitor and will grow well from bare soils to produce a thick bed of rich green stingers. Not only are they essential to ensure that all stages of this species prosper on your patch but they are also a fantastic environment for a whole community of other non butterfly invertebrates at various valuable levels in the healthier garden's food chain.

BEING REALISTIC ABOUT YOUR SPACE

Perhaps the greatest enemy of your objectives is idealism. As a child I implored my parents to recreate one of those fashionable gardens, perfectly and quite impractically illustrated in various brightly coloured publications – striped lawns, rosy pergolas, straight fences, lobate borders and neat patios. Naturally our garden was too small, too narrow and cluttered with irritations like garages, coal bunkers, fruit trees, a wood pile, not to mention my camps and my sister's discarded Spacehopper, none of which were ever included in the 'Gardens for you' sections of my grandfather's gardening magazines. So, admit your limitations, analyse them in detail, and turn any negatives into positives by focusing upon what you really can achieve rather than what it would be nice to do.

You could try to plant a grouse moor on the dry soils of a Semi-D in Southwark, or put up an Osprey nesting platform in Truro town centre. Flooding fifty square

Left: *Chaos, marvellous chaos. A riot of unconstrained growth going wild, and sadly not every gardener's cup of tea.*

metres of suburban Inverness and seeding a reedbed won't save the imperilled Bittern, even if it is your favourite bird. In '*Magnum Force*' Clint Eastwood says, 'A man's gotta know his limitations'. Forget the gender directive – it's true! But also in this instance complicated by your neighbours and your neighbourhood's limitations. For instance, if you have the only large garden complete with a few large trees on Brighton sea front, I'd forget about catering for Nuthatches, Hedgehogs, or Pine Martens. But if you have a tiny garden which backs onto extensive broad-leaved woodland in central England, I'd prime the nut feeder and put some cat food out on the lawn each evening. And if your minuscule patch happens to be lost in the ruins of Scotland's ancient Caledonian forest, I'd try a few strawberry jam sandwiches on the bird table – apparently Pine Martens love them! I'm sure you get the picture.

Know Your Neighbourhood

Take a wander out one evening, be a bit nosey, see if the Smeggits in number 10 still have that big ivy-covered sycamore. Peer over the fence, the Bests may have two noisy boys in Man United shirts but they've got a huge pond. And see if Mr Bloveld across the road still has that horrible fluffy cat. How far away exactly is that bramble-strewn wasteland? Is old Barry next door still spending 95% of his pension on slug pellets in a single-handed assault on the Mollusca? Has Sheila's recent appointment at the local concrete company paid dividends in her attempt to fabricate a patio that can be seen from space? Of course, in a country where a house is a castle, none of this is any of your business, but it will have a profound effect on what could be coaxed over your moat and into your keep. Your neighbour's peculiarities are

Above: *Decorative yes, non-native species certainly, but nevertheless a bountiful supply of nectar which is a basic requirement for so many insect species. This alone means that a window box qualifies as a wildlife reserve.*

Above and left: *What a fantastic garden! I wish it were mine. Obviously the work of a dedicated wildlife lover, but if yours is a smaller patch don't worry. The habitat adjacent to the blocks below will be a rich source of species which could easily be attracted to lower floor window boxes.*

and the acidity/alkalinity of your potential pondwater. Sunshine hours and aspect you might have dwelt upon when placing barbecues, patios, conservatories, or merely deckchairs. Unfortunately, all these 'secondaries' do need a modicum or more of thought. Some important plants have uncompromising requirements in terms of the soil and its drainage where they are rooted, and light and shade where their leaves hang. The good news is twofold: one, many of these requirements and their intricacies are known and the information is relatively accessible. Thus you can choose and cultivate successfully. Two, if you have a small garden or a small area you can probably modify it by draining or flooding, and or by digging out and replacing the soil. But beware, this could be a big, messy, unpopular and expensive initial step. But then if you want heather because you want lizards, who am I to dampen your desire for dry well drained and impoverished acidic soil by the truckload?

your considerations when it comes to conservation. Have a word with Barry though, try to slow up his genocide, show him photos of happy Hedgehogs and smiling Slow-worms – and if all this fails, tell him about the lottery!

Right, now you've considered the surface topography you'll have to get a bit more physical. Soil types, are not a fascination for many, nor are drainage patterns, hydrology,

ALL AROUND YOUR PLACE

A great distance from the nearest 'big trees' may also be limiting when it comes to attracting woodland birds such as the tits, nuthatches and woodpeckers

Lots of 'sterile' housing with very little greenery between you and the wider countryside will not help. Some of the stronger flying, bolder or tenacious species will reach you but too much concrete will slow them up or rule them out altogether.

Spread the word. Try and involve your neighbours and community in conservation by gently persuading them to consider the impact they can really have on their environment. The best way to get someone to feed the birds is to invite them round and show them what you've got over a coffee, a beer or a barbecue. Enthusiasm is often infectious!

Unfortunately a neighbour's cat will have a profound effect on your garden's fauna and how you seek to encourage and manage it. There is no doubt that a cat-free garden is a healthier environment all round but achieving this is not easy. Try some of the ultrasonic deterrents and at the very least politely enquire if the animal might be collared with a double bell or new techno alarm collar: maybe this would be an ideal Christmas present for the moggy's owner!

Proximity to a patch of 'wasteland' is probably the ultimate bonus. Undisturbed and unmanaged scrub is likely to become a great natural sourcing ground for many species: everything from hedgehogs to butterflies, beetles, maybe even slow worms and foxes. Try to look after it too!

The privacy of railway embankments and their relative lack of management means that they can act as great wildlife corridors, allowing species to creep, blow or be carried from the countryside deep into suburbia or even the city. Roe Deer may well keep clear of the A 372 but have no fear in sneaking through the seclusion of these overgrown rail routes.

Proximity to any watercourse, however sad or small, will prove an invaluable asset when it comes to the natural colonisation of your pond. Many species will use rivers and streams as routes as they disperse across the country and will fan out from them and hopefully find your new resource. Of course with some species of commoner and more resilient plants and animals they are an ideal local source of specimens. Before you pack your pond net and bucket be sure to consider the ethics and potential effectiveness of your translocations.

Old hedgerows, relics of countryside left in the town are an invaluable source of specialist species, those that require a little more than a quick fix of Buddleia or bowl of table scraps.

Minor roads are not a problem. Actual casualties will be few and many of the larger animals use them to get around. Major roads are bad news. Avoid As and Ms.

The ideal neighbour! Okay it's ordered, but there are sizeable trees, plenty of nectar bearing flowers, some cover in the form of creepers, a bird table, nest boxes and the major bonus of a pond with a wildlife slant. This has the potential to be a good suburban refuge and by living near it you will undoubtedly benefit. Of course when some of your own objectives are recognised the benefit will be mutual and if enthusiasm spreads to some more of your neighbours the whole community will rapidly improve as a wildlife resource.

Noisy children next door are actually not the end of the world when it comes to wildlife. Firstly they are only active when out of school and in good weather and daylight, and secondly unless they are 'airgun assassins' they are unlikely to harm very much. Shyer species may stay away until they go away, so secretive species such as foxes and badgers will simply adjust their arrival times accordingly. Remember, rather than scorning them you could invite them round to watch and learn!

CONSIDER YOUR ASPECT

Consider your aspect. Now there's some advice! But when it's followed with a suggestion that before you get started with any wildlife gardening you think about drainage, soil type, slope and position relative to neighbours, the postulation becomes practical rather than philosophical.

The single most important external influence upon your future plans is sunlight. Thus the direction that your house and/or garden faces relative to the sun will have a profound effect upon many things, not least heat and light for growth. There's is no point in planting sunflowers in the shade, but if shade is what you've got there are plenty of equally productive species that will attract and provide for a similar range of animals.

If you would like insects – bugs, beetles, bees and butterflies – to buzz around your place then you'll need to set them up with a few nectar-filled suntraps. A buddleia bush in the shade would not only be a little straggly but also deserted of life. When you're planning or planting consider this carefully; it is unlikely that your resource will be in shade all day long. You may need a 'morning bush' and an 'afternoon bush' and remember that other creatures such as lizards and some birds also have a keen affinity for our big yellow star.

Other considerations are soil type and drainage. It's normally easier to make it drier than wetter which is a shame because a mosaic of soil moisture could be highly desirable

Left: *My mother says, 'There's rarely any substitute for hard work'. Unfortunately, my mother's rarely wrong.*

if you plan for a pond and accompanying marshy fringes. Most modern gardens of average size will be well or too well drained, an artefact of the building process, and to get water back into the ground will almost certainly require an external source, that is a tap with a flow organized or paid for by you. If you are not on a meter then consider this and don't feel too guilty about it being a 'waste'. You can also conserve a lot of useful 'garden-water' by installing water butts under all of your drainpipes and if you're fanatical and do it with a series of butts you could store enough to see a modest garden through summer droughts. If you plan major drainage I'd advise liaison with a hydrologist.

Above: *Put peat in your garden and I'll never speak to you again!*

Soil type is more easily manipulated as you can buy a few cubic metres of almost all soils from alkaline to acidic and put it wherever you like. Thus it is easy to alter the soil profile of your garden and there are few gardens that wouldn't benefit from this. Many new houses have a very thin, indeed a mean layer of top soil spread over gravel and builders' rubble. You'll be better off by raking this away, digging the rubbish out and shifting a lot more and a lot better soil in. It will be messy and back breaking, but will certainly pay dividends in the end.

Improving your soil with peat is of course a complete non starter. Peat bogs are incredibly endangered habitats and due to gardeners' demand for peat nearly all have been destroyed in the UK. Peat-free composting materials are widely available. The B & Q chain is very active with this initiative but the Wildlife Trusts will provide details of where to buy peat-free products (see page 140).

Above: *Phone 'soil supplies' immediately – or get a few cacti and a rattlesnake – this ground needs help.*

PLANNING PERMISSION

O kay, it's post-*Neighbours*, pre-*Top of the Pops*, and you've made a special effort rejecting microchips for something actually cookable and possibly even edible from Delia's latest. It's gone down well. Now is the time to tell them.

The lawn's going. It's going to be a wild flower meadow. The patio is set to be a six point feeding station for birds, so sorry, 'Tibbles' is retiring to the Blue Cross. The shed, well, that's a nettle bed waiting to happen. Aunt Vera's Magnolia doesn't have a preservation order, and nor do the two 'non-native' borders. The barbecue is in the balance: it's a good spot for the swamp. The nation's wildlife needs us, we must unite to save the newt!

Expect a public enquiry. Or sit-ins. Your partner chained to the aforementioned Magnolia won't look good if the boss sees it in the local Press. Thus I must advise discourse, diplomacy, and democracy. In reality we all share spaces. So sue for the best amenable compromise, don't confuse 10 feet with 10 metres when it comes to the cut, tolerate the few begonias (great slug food anyhow!) and try to win any opponents over with stonking views of your first successes. Give them full on male Great Spotted Woodpeckers ten feet from the dining room table. Show them frolicking fox cubs for supper. See them enthuse, see the barbecue fall, watch gleefully as they flood the vegetable patch in anticipation of a plague of amphibians. Or pray they tolerate your eccentricities!

Above: Pit bulls in a china shop? Not really, because ball games rarely last the full ninety minutes in the garden, and by tea-time the wildlife will have its day. And to be fair, like it or not, it's their space too.

Follow the Rules

Of course, on a moderately more serious note are the legal planning constraints imposed by your local council. Tree preservation orders are under used and over abused – be careful when chainsawing a glade, in some places the maximum fine is £20,000 per tree. Conservation areas are popular and can be a useful method of unifying the appearance of a neighbourhood in which they apply. They are not actually a nuisance, but act as a guideline to try to maintain the aspect of an area, both in terms of its architecture, its aesthetic resource and its environmental value. Indeed, even some environmental improvements can counter the rules here, but such problems are easily overcome for the trouble of a phone call to the planning officers in charge. They will generally politely discuss your proposals, and if they are perceived as in any way radical pay a visit to understand the reality. When all is straight, you apply for permission, and if your neighbours don't disapprove too violently and your plan fits in the general scheme of things, you progress. Please don't let fear of this process tempt you to plough ahead without notification. Aside from simply not being fair, it would be a real misery to have to undo all your hard work. If your plans are on the 'Grand Scale' then so must be your preparatory work. Drainage changes might sink your neighbour's foundations, and earth-moving equipment wake their baby. As usual consult experts and use a combination of common sense and good manners to combat any potential conflict. It will always help if your neighbours learn to enjoy your wildlife as much as you do. If you annoy them in the process it may be very counter-productive in the long run.

BIRDS

BACK GARDEN BIRDING

A curious and unfortunate affliction, which grips many serious ornithologists, is the need to keep lists. Not content to document all the birds they've seen in Britain, or indeed the world, some fanatics even keep lists of birds they've seen on television or in zoological collections. Whilst such obsessions border on lunacy, I think it's fairly reasonable to keep a note of all the species that one encounters in the garden. And over a few years you'll be surprised by quite how many different types of birds you might be able to find. One acquaintance of mine who keeps such a garden list has spotted Buzzard, Hobby, Merlin, Bewick's Swan, Red-breasted Merganser and Yellow-browed Warbler. He lives no more than a mile and a half from the centre of Southampton in a densely populated suburb. Bill Oddie once had a garden that over looked the ponds on Hampstead Heath and watched Greenshank flying over. Within his fenced boundaries he also enjoyed Redstart, Pied Flycatcher and, quite extraordinarily, a singing Wood Warbler. For my part I once had the good fortune to have a flat which over looked a river and during the dreary second half of an FA Cup Final, glanced out of the window to notice an Osprey. The real highlight however was a Nightjar which one evening flew up the river at low tide and was quite evidently lost, flying as it was north when it should have been flying south to Africa!

Of course these are exotic exceptions, the real gems of lists which have taken between five and ten years to note. But most city gardens should over a period of time produce somewhere between fifty and eighty different species. Many garden species are refugees from woodland clearings and edges and they successfully endure a noisy cat ridden existence in our gardens because the structure of these often closely matches the vegetational layers found in woodland. Ground, herb and shrub layers, understoreys and canopies even composed of introduced species, provide a replica of their natural foraging and nesting grounds. What's more, any food shortages can be alleviated by one of our national obsessions: the great British bird table.

Left: *The perfect antidote to a nil-nil draw, a view of an Osprey out of the dining room window (sadly it didn't stay for extra time!).*

As you might expect eccentricity runs riot, not only through the design of bird tables, everything from gothic castle, Tudor and thatched cottages, post modernist blocks and even a few 'monstrous carbunkles', but also with regard to their menus. Fish and chips for Starlings, haggis for Crested Tits, hot-cross buns for Mute Swans and egg custards for Moorhens. The national cuisine is stretched to the limits! The best bird I ever saw coming to a table was no less than a Water Rail, a customer to one avian restaurant *par excellence*; a floating feeding platform on someone's garden pond! Generally bread is the most frequently provided food, but it has one third of the energy of fat and you should be careful about feeding dry, stale bread to breeding birds; it can easily become stuck in the throats of their young. Always provide plenty of water as well as food. The same applies to desiccated coconut, although fresh bisected coconuts hung upside down provide a welcome alternative to some of the more acrobatic visitors, perhaps the most common of which are the tits. Some of these species spend up to ninety-seven percent of their winter's daylight just searching for food, obviously a critical factor affecting their survival. Bird tables are also very valuable as a whole, because believe or not, more than fifty individual Blue Tits probably visit your platform or your feeders. A maximum of a hundred and forty-eight have been recorded and many of these are actually entirely dependant on bird table food. Without it, it's thought that up to fifty percent of garden birds would probably die.

So recognize your responsibility, consider the options in terms of diets and methods of delivering them. Keep your binoculars and notebooks at the ready, and stray no further than your dining room or kitchen window to enjoy the best things in life – birds!

DELIVERING THE DIET

As I write, there are about ten to fifteen Great Tits, a similar number of Blue Tits, at least one Marsh or Willow Tit, a couple of Coal Tits, eight Chaffinches, five or six Greenfinches, a pair of Goldfinches, two Robins, a Dunnock, a Blackbird, a single Collared Dove and at least three Nuthatches on or around our patio. Every ten minutes a Jay pops up for some loose peanuts, and normally once a day a Sparrowhawk tries its luck. I have to say that these birds are not personal friends of mine, I am not living in a Technicolor Disney cartoon where all the birds, bees and beasts love me. No, the cold cruel facts are that they're all here because I feed them every day of the year. Our rectangle of concrete is the neighbourhood's McDonalds for birds. They know the menu, the prices and the best seats. The regularity of opening hours always guarantees a packed restaurant, there's no door policy – squirrels, of which there are currently two – are welcome on the ground but not on the feeders which they destroy. The Sparrowhawk is welcome too – I am happy to lose a few customers to anything that beautiful.

Fundamentally a bird feeder equates to a permanently fruiting tree. If it's filled all year and not only enriched for a short period it is, in all honesty, better than that which nature provided. What's more it's an instantly mature tree. You buy, fill, and site it and it's ready for action. No seedling, maturing or years of waiting for five or six berries. No, it's Wham – Big Food Source – wherever you want it! With a modicum of ingenuity you can place your feeder wherever it's best for the birds and for you. Safe from predators but easy to see. And of course for a few pounds more you can appeal to different species

Left: *A commercially available peanut feeder that will ensure that only the birds get the food. Narrow gaps between the bars also selects which species can squeeze through. Yes to tits, no to Starlings.*

Above: *A little twee, but at least it is delivering the goods. At the end of the day it doesn't matter how smart or how scruffy a bird table is: so long as it is safely sited and regularly loaded with grub, no birds will turn up their beaks!*

by getting a second feeder and filling it with a different food, maybe up-market types such as Siskins, Long-tailed Tits, Woodpeckers or those dapper Nuthatches – my favourites!

Ground or Table

The simplest feeding station is the ground, but there are two problems with scattering food on your lawn. Firstly, not only birds will be able to access the food. Dogs, cats, foxes, badgers, squirrels, hedgehogs and, less savoury for some, rats and mice, will all have free access to your fare. Secondly, not all birds like to feed on the ground – thrushes, finches, pigeons, robins, magpies and jays regularly do, and tits will, but they prefer not to. They are tree-feeding types and don't feel safe down that low.

The simplest solution is the bird table, a flat platform which is raised to reduce the mammalian interest. Cover it and the food will last longer in the relative dry; make a tray of it and the food won't all blow onto the ground in the wind.

Again a range of species will use it, but some won't enjoy it, and if they don't then you won't either. Faced with a plate of peanuts or sunflower seeds all the tit species will fly up, pinch one and then fly off to some cover to eat it – all you'll see is a flash of blue and a whirr of wings. The answer is to shop for specialist feeders and there are hundreds to choose from.

From a Feeder

Traditionally, the peanut basket is a favourite. This wire mesh tube prevents the removal of the whole nut and ensures that the clientele stick around pecking at it whilst you get to watch them. Feeders and baskets come in all shapes and sizes, but must be protected from squirrels which easily gnaw them open to feast on the feast that falls. Plastic shields beneath supporting poles or slippery domes suspended above those that hang will normally do the trick, as will the heavy duty caging that surrounds the interior nut dispenser of some models, (see opposite) Nevertheless, never underestimate the persistence, the ingenuity, or the damnable destructive capability of Mr Nutkin.

Other Options

Various essentially similar devices dispense seeds or mixes through port holes in the sides and come in simple, easy to maintain utilitarian plastic or rustic or posh ceramic forms, some too decorative to effectively dispense anything other than pretension!

Some of the better models also come in a choice of colours, typically silver, black, red, green and blue. This is not to match the patio paintwork but has been proven to attract different species at different times of the year. Regional differences seem to apply, so if you fancy some really simple science get yourself a notebook, a pencil, stopwatch, calculator and a few pots of paint. You never know, you might prove that some Blue Tits are colour blind!

If like me, you believe that the best things in life are birds, then you'll need to think big. Big feeders stock more food so they need to be less regularly filled and will satisfy a bigger flock. Mine, he says bragging, can hold 6.4 kg, that's 14 lb. of food and it's got sixteen feeding ports and basically it's a case of, 'Go ahead Greenfinch – make my day!' Needless to say, these monster feeders need a good heavy base for support. But you know when it comes to feeders, big is still not the best.

Plastic suckers are the tops when it comes to feeding birds. No longer attached to toy arrows or Garfield's feet (think about it), they now serve to stick peanut, seed, multipurpose and live food feeders to your window, which means that the diners are all but in the room with you. Birds take a little while to get used to them but if you stand still you'll not get better views of your best friends. A few tips: 1) Don't economise on the quality of sticker, if they don't stick you'll be forever sweeping up seed on the windowsill, and the birds will never feel safely perched; 2) Don't go for those which have a water trough as well as a food tray. The first dirty bather to squeeze in and shake off renders everything else invisible, and 3) Beware of Collared Doves. They are too heavy and too flappy for even the strongest suckers and will tear your feeders from the glass. Stick it where they won't or can't reach.

Left: *A fully loaded feeder complete with five fans no doubt a little fatter for their endeavours.*

Below: *The fanatic in action – if they can't get enough, then nor can I, and remember regularity is the key to keeping them coming.*

WHEN, WHAT AND WHO TO FEED

I am always being asked: 'Should we feed our birds all year?' At some time it must have been frowned upon to do so, but not now. Our garden birds have become sorry refugees from a ruined countryside. In the last twenty-five years the intensification of agriculture has ravaged our rural bird populations – Skylarks down by 50%, Tree Sparrows by 90%, even House Sparrow numbers have collapsed. Combine this with the urbanizing of the countryside, building around our town and city fringes, with pollution through the overuse of pest and herbicides, plus over extraction of water, and it is clear that rural Britain has become a difficult place for wildlife to prosper. It's not an overstatement to say, 'Your birds need you'. If we all stopped feeding the birds tomorrow the effect would be catastrophic. If twice as many of us put food out it would be remarkable. So yes, yes, yes – please feed the birds all year round!

Let's consider the benefits to the birds. Firstly, because they are small and have high metabolic rates most garden birds need to consume between twenty-five and fifty per cent of their body weight every day. In winter, when foraging time is restricted by the shorter day length, Blue Tits need to find food every twelve to fifteen seconds. Things are tough out there on the patio, so it's

Left: Naughty boy's appetite for apple produces a guilty look. Still, share and share alike?

important that the right choices are made. They need it fast, but 'burgers and fries' are not enough for our birds; they need balanced diets.

Peanuts

Peanuts are not actually nuts - they grow in the ground and are more like lentils and peas. High in proteins, oils and calories, they are ideal for the smaller species such as Blue and Coal Tits. In recent years somewhat exaggerated reports have appeared in the Press about peanut poisoning. Aflatoxin is the problem and while it is rare it's also real, so buy good quality peanuts. If you wouldn't eat them yourself maybe you shouldn't offer them to the birds!

Sunflower Seeds

Sunflower seeds have a very high oil content, and de-husked sunflower hearts are tops in terms of calories. Black sunflower seeds are even better than the standard 'striped seeds' as they have even more oil. Again these are great for the little burners of the bird table, Blue and Coal Tits.

Cereals

Oats, normally rolled, or even de-husked and crushed into pinhead oats are high in carbohydrates but not so oily or so rich in calories. Mixed corn is what many ground-feeding birds used to get in our farmed fields. It's okay as a staple, but even with maize added doesn't rival the oil-rich sunflower seeds.

Left: Water is often in shorter supply than food, so both drinking and bathing water are essential and should be regularly replenished all year round. Here a heater prevents winter freezing and keeps a bathing Song Thrush happy.

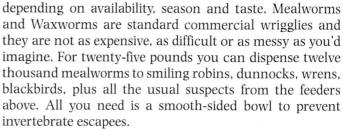

Raisins and Sultanas

Moderate energy for fruit-favouring species. Best scattered onto the ground or piled onto the bird table as they are too sticky to go in a feeder.

Nyjer Seeds

This 'new' food finds its way into many seed mixes where it is a valuable oil-rich energy-giving item. Sometimes it's called 'thistle seed' which it isn't, but it can be used to attract Goldfinches to specialized feeders – that's if the more resourceful Greenfinches don't get in first.

Seed Mixes

These products are the best option by far as they combine all of the above items in a balanced formula to attract a wide range of birds to a single feeder. The best brands contain black sunflower seeds, sunflower hearts, peanut granules, kibbled maize, pinhead oatmeal, canary seed, millet and hemp.

Table Scraps

Don't waste these and never leave a restaurant without a Foxie or Birdie bag. (These were formerly known as Doggie bags, but since some restaurants probably seat dogs themselves these days they are no longer required for our canine friends.) There will be something in your scraps to suit something outside, even if it's mice, slugs, or next door's cat. I put all ours on a raised platform each night; this keeps the 'mess' in one place and allows me to see what's eating them, either by watching or checking for footprints. Feeding on a raised table may also reduce the likelihood of attracting rats, whereas if you throw everything directly to the ground you are inviting these rodents to dinner.

Fat Products

Suet is not cool. Lard is now laughable! No darlings, it's Extra Virgin Olive Oil for us. But the birds like the old-fashioned stuff. Lard and suet cakes infused with peanut flour, seeds or whatever you've got, hung up on bits of string, are a Blue Peter regular and they work brilliantly. Fat is a superb source of concentrated energy. Aside from the usual tits and greedy Starlings you'll stand a chance of attracting Nuthatches and even Treecreepers, Long-tailed tits and Goldcrests. If your kids are growing up and not making 'bird cakes' they are being deprived, and so are the birds!

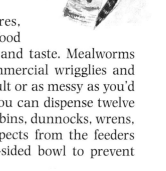

Live Foods

Most garden birds are omnivores, enjoying both animal and plant food depending on availability, season and taste. Mealworms and Waxworms are standard commercial wrigglies and they are not as expensive, as difficult or as messy as you'd imagine. For twenty-five pounds you can dispense twelve thousand mealworms to smiling robins, dunnocks, wrens, blackbirds, plus all the usual suspects from the feeders above. All you need is a smooth-sided bowl to prevent invertebrate escapees.

Practicalities

Shop for bird food to combine value for money with ease of collection. Mail Order is the best option because you can arrange deliveries of specific foods at competitive prices, and this will allow you to keep a ready stock of food, which is very important.

I once ran out of bird food. It took me ten to fourteen days to organize new stock and refill the feeders, and nearly two months for the number of birds to recover. My Nuthatches vanished until the next winter, no doubt having located another more reliable feeder elsewhere. A disaster!

Of course stock means storage. I use plastic dustbins, although if your dry storage space is not rodent proof I'd go for the metal equivalent to prevent mice from being too tempted. Dryness is essential because any moisture seems to increase the risk of mite infestation.

Cleanliness is critical and incidences of *Salmonella* and *E.coli* seem to be on the up. Large concentrations of birds sharing the same feeders mean infections spread rapidly and soon dead or dying birds will litter the garden. Avoid such unpleasantness by cleaning beneath feeders, sweeping the bird table and disinfecting it and all the feeders and water dispensers, at least three or four times a year. If food remains uneaten or goes mouldy, dispose of it carefully and quickly.

The Science of Feeding Birds

You may consider this a pretentious title but you'd be wrong – nutrition is a very serious science, and an understanding of avian nutrition may be set to save a number of threatened British species. But I'm not an expert; Chris Whittles is. A lifelong interest in birds led him first to bird ringing, on to a position as the Honorary Secretary of the British Trust for Ornithology, and then in 1987 to start a company, C.J. Wildbird Foods Limited. Both as a businessman and as a scientist he recognised a gap in the market. Thirty million pounds a year was being spent on birdfood, but it was generally cereal-based, high in carbohydrate but low in energy; not very rewarding for birds. Chris felt that he could improve the product and turn a profit too, and he wasn't wrong.

Chris' research technique is simple. He sources new foods, puts them out in the garden and waits to see what eats them. He trials his mixes at home and then in a series of gardens around the UK where keen observers record their local birds' reaction to the new dishes. If something finds favour it is analysed for energetic value and Chris begins a global search for the very best quality ingredients.

As any good restaurateur will tell you, presentation can be everything, and when C.J.'s were first trying Nyjer seed they sourced a specific feeder from America. It had small slots cut in it to allow Goldfinches, the target species, to pick the seed out. Chris didn't have a slot cutter, so he drilled holes instead and when the new device was tested an observer reported that the birds looked uncomfortable. So

Above: *Chris Whittles, a commercial conservationist committed to developing practical technology to help birds. The Barnes Wallis of the Bird table! Where's his O.B.E.?*

the holes were raised, offset from the perches, and it worked.

In the UK no fewer than seventy nine species have been recorded using C.J. feeders or food. Spotted Flycatchers supplement their nestlings' diet on mealworms, Turtle Doves pick up Nyjer that Goldfinches have spilled and, remarkably, Sedge Warblers, Chiffchaffs, Willow Warblers and Goldcrests have benefited from fat bars filled with dead insects. Best of all though are the Corn Buntings, Cirl Buntings, Skylarks and Tree Sparrows which are now regularly enjoying a special high energy groundbird mix which includes those all-important sunflower hearts. When the RSPB initiated a Cirl Bunting recovery programme a few years ago they came to Chris and asked him to prepare a barley and grass seed mix. He did, but he was sceptical. OK the birds used to eat this, but they didn't exactly profit – they were critically endangered after all. A new 'artificial' blend was tried and now the Cirl Bunting is all but clear of danger and for the first time in a century spreading its range.

Research continues; recently, dyeing sunflower hearts red was found to attract Blackcaps to them, and by replacing *Dendrobaena* worms with *Lumbricus* species, Song Thrushes have also been tempted.

Chris also researches his human customers, and the good news is that most people no longer feed their birds just for fun; everyone realises there is a conservation concern today. The bad news is that most of his customers are aged from their mid 40s upwards, so come on you young, have a heart and shell out for a few sunflower seeds for the birds!

FEEDING EXOTICS

Not satisfied with Nuthatches? Bored with Blue Tits? Great Tits not grabbing your fancy? Then you need some exotic interests and if you're lucky there might be something in the neighbourhood for you.

In recent years a number of new species have been tempted to the bird table. Blackcaps, now known to over-winter here regularly, will nick morsels from the table or even perch on the fat-cake. Bullfinches, starved out of the countryside, have started to nibble seeds and peanuts as have Goldfinches, Yellowhammers and Linnets. Long-tailed Tits, Goldcrests and even those dinky little jewels, Firecrests, have said yes to the ambitious chef, but then once ambition gets started, it knows no bounds.

Ring-necked Parakeets, those escaped pets and former residents of Asia and aviaries from South London to Kent, now roam widely from Henley to Margate and south to Hampshire, Surrey, Sussex and Southern Kent, not to mention most of South London. Initially they were held in check by a few stiff winters but now noisy flocks of five hundred plus can be seen flying to roost and also descending onto a few select bird tables. I visited a lady's garden in Sandwich in Kent where every day for the price of some Granny Smiths and a couple of over-ripe Coxes a colourful cabaret of these brilliant green and rose-pink exotics descended to brighten the winter's gloom. It was a fabulous treat, and one that could be available to millions of southern bird lovers.

Even more ambitious are those raptor enthusiasts who have invested in a large freezer and filled it full of 'hatchery offal', the rather ungracious name for all the dead male day-old chicks that will never 'enjoy' life in the battery farms of Britain. These become a valuable food source for many zoos and falconers and make a neat bite size treat for everything from Buzzards,

Sparrowhawks, Kestrels and Tawny Owls, all of which I've seen visiting special feeding platforms across the UK. The Buzzards were daily guests at a ten-metre high table which was loaded by a rope pulley and bucket system, thus avoiding the need for extending the ladder. Six chicks, defrosted at dawn and served at nine-thirty a.m. led to a despicable display of table manners between the mild but more minor male and a fatter foul-tempered female – great value!

Another gentleman in Berkshire has a similar table, albeit lacking in a dumb waiter, something he's made up for with the practised ability to pitch a yellow fluffy chick with pinpoint accuracy. Its particular nifty addition is a forty watt, well weatherproofed lamp. Here it's not breakfast for Buzzards, but a case of supper for the local Tawny Owls which arrive and depart quickly, silently but no doubt gratefully after their free first course of the evening. It's all over in an instant but his photographs are superb.

Pheasants, Fieldfares, Green Woodpeckers, even Crested Tits and Grey Wagtails have been tempted onto tables across the UK. See what you've got in the neighbourhood, pick up the book to check what it eats and devise a realistic alternative to its diet, followed by a means of preparing and presenting the dish. All you have to do then is sit back and wait. Remember, few of us will say no to a free meal!

BIRD NESTING BOXES

All your attention is focused on a small black hole cut in the front of a little wooden box pinned onto the garage. Did you see a bird go in, or did you just imagine it? The trouble is you really want to see a bird going in, in fact you may want it so much you might imagine it. Minutes tick by and you're still focused on that tiny black circle. You turn around to get a biscuit and – Oh, what was that? No, was that a bird that flew out? Damn! You'll have to keep watching, you can't go out and lift the lid, because if there is a Blue Tit in that nest box it might fly off and not come back and you don't want to imagine anything as bad as that.

There is something intrinsically satisfying about building a home for a bird, waiting to see it chosen and then watching a family raised and fledged from it. Something fascinating about the birds' speed and tenacity throughout the process and something simply awesome about their dedication and energy. And from a bird's point of view it's a bonus too. I mean, you've been feeding them all winter, you've lured them into suburbia with an endless diet of top treats, but now, when the business starts, when they get the essential urge, where are they going to do it? The problem, as ever, is the 'too tidy' phenomenon.

New Niches Needed

Because so many of our 'garden birds' are woodland species that have gone over to the 'urban side', and because in food-rich areas their population can increase to higher levels than those found in their native habitats, there will always be a shortage of nesting sites. The avian housing problem is exacerbated by our preoccupation with 'over-gardening' and removing too much dead wood, our misplaced hatred of ivy with its sheltering and secret niche forming habits, and our sterile modern house building styles that leave no cracks in the eves or crannies in the brick work. And it's not just our gardens, it's all around the neighbourhood – in our parks, public areas, patches of 'wasteland' or whatever. With

Above left, above and below: *Some species prefer a little secrecy – Tawny Owls and Robins are cases in point – whilst Blue Tits can be brazen box fillers and do the business right in front of your window. Here a fledgling peeps out on a wider world.*

an obvious shortage of mature trees what hope is there for a Blue Tit finding an unoccupied hole, a Robin finding a crack beneath a bough, a Flycatcher discovering a cleft in the ivy, let alone a Starling squeezing under a loose roof tile or a Swift skimming into an entrance to a nice dry loft. That's why when last spring I put up eighteen nest boxes in our garden, super saturation I might add as it's not that large, by the end of the breeding season nine had been used, eight successfully. That's nine nest sites that weren't previously available, immediately snapped up by the homeless of Netley, Southampton. More importantly, it's twenty-seven more Blue Tits, nine more Great Tits and four more Robins than fledged in our garden the year before we moved in.

Over the years enthusiasts have designed nest boxes and platforms for almost every species you can think of. From Willow Tits to Ospreys; from Little Terns to Long-eared Owls; from Goldeneyes to Goldcrests. And it continues.

While Jim Flegg's *Nest Boxes* first published by the BTO in 1971 is still an industry standard, recently the Hawk and Owl Trust's *Birds Boxes and Baskets* has helped raptor enthusiasts, and an increasingly ingenious array of commercially available boxes has provided the DIY–challenged amateur with an instant answer to the dearth of natural nesting sites.

Wood or Not?

Traditionally nest boxes have always been wooden affairs, some over indulging design and of little use to any bird, others being so rustic that rustic was rapidly replaced by rotten! With today's pressure-treated timbers there is no excuse for the latter, so simply shop for a sturdy, practical and easy to clean box and expect to spend somewhere between seven and twenty pounds. If you're cool you'll make sure the timber came from sustainably harvested forests – otherwise it simply means you're indirectly doing someone else out of a home somewhere else in the world. However, purists would say that wood has had its day. Increasingly popular are wood-crete boxes. These 'prefab' homes are made from a secret mix of concrete and sawdust which allows the box to breathe and thus reduces both condensation and humidity. It's said that research has shown that birds prefer these boxes, that more young are fledged and that they'll last a lifetime. I once plagiarised Prince Charles on national television and called these boxes 'monstrous carbuncles' and as a consequence was much chastised. Call me old fashioned but I think they look awful, so I'll stick with my DIY pine plank, my Spear and Jackson ripsaw, a few screws and some scentless creosote, thank you, and anyway nine out of eighteen in one year isn't bad is it?

Siting nest boxes is critical and yet very difficult to provide precise guidelines for. This is simply because no two gardens are the same and aside from the basic common sense required you'll just have to experiment. Two things to remember are shelter from wind, rain and strong sunlight, and safety in terms of predators, particularly cats. You should combine consideration based upon these

Left and below: No cavities in your neat brick work? Then give a fly-catcher, wagtail, robin or sparrow a little space filler at the cost of twenty-five minutes of DIY.

requirements with your desire to witness the breeding show and a need to clean out the box. The latter couldn't be simpler – pull out all the old nesting material in the autumn, scrape or brush out any residues and effect any external repairs. If you do get a problem with cats then perhaps the 'Nest Box Guardian' might help. Marketed by CJ Wildbird Foods, this device is a stout plastic tube which clips into, and tightens onto the nest hole, to effectively stop cats clawing at the entrance. If squirrels or Great Spotted Woodpeckers are the foe, steel plates with holes of an identical diameter screwed onto the face of the box will at least slow, if not stifle an attack on the occupants. One last tip, if a box is not used in one year don't be afraid to move it in the winter and try a new spot the next spring, a few feet can sometimes make all the difference to our more fickle feathered friends.

Left: All systems go in the Packham 'Tit rehabilitation programme'. My girlfriend's dad, Richard, made this beauty and the Great Tits were in after ten minutes.

Below: Try for Treecreepers with this specialized design.

BIRD NESTING BOXES

Top Tips

- Pressure-treated timber largely negates the need to paint the finished box with any wood preservative. However, most pressure-treated timbers seem to be honey-coloured or green, so if you wish your boxes to blend in a little more an extra coat of staining preservative in dark oak or chestnut may be necessary, but remember only treat the exterior of the box, never the inside.

- Make sure the timber is at least 2 cm thick to provide good insulation and to avoid warping and splitting.

- Use brass or plated screws and clips to facilitate repair or maintenance.

- With the exception of the entrance hole diameters these dimensions are only a guide; they do not need to be religiously adhered to, cut your box according to what you have available, the birds are not often that discerning!

- Screwing or nailing a box to a tree is not a sensible option if the tree is ever likely to be felled. When chainsaw meets metal, catastrophe and serious injury can result. An alternative is to use wooden pegs or dowels. Usually made from teak, beech or oak, these can be hammered into slightly undersized holes drilled in the tree. Fixing to walls, wooden or brick, should be done as solidly as possible. Birds don't like wobbly boxes!

- Most boxes should be sited between two and five metres in height, but of course their position should be predominantly determined by inaccessibility to predators (cats, squirrels, mice and rats), and the local climate. Do not place it in too exposed a position or with the entrance hole facing the wind or tilted upwards, or too close to another box — leave a distance of about 10 m.

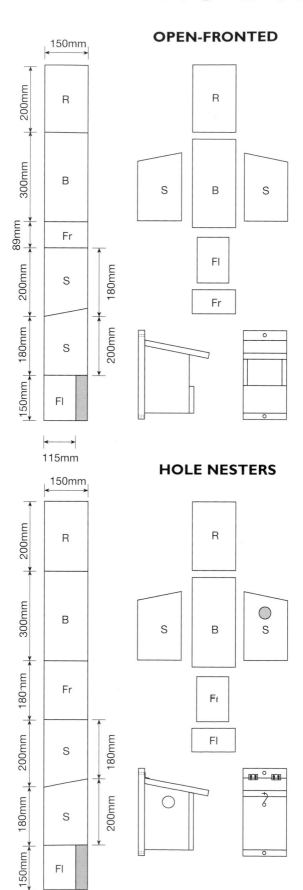

OPEN-FRONTED

HOLE NESTERS

Size of hole	Species
25mm	Blue Tit, Coal Tit, Marsh Tit
32mm	Pied Flycatcher, Great Tit, Nuthatch, Tree Sparrow
200mm	Stock Dove, Tawny Owl, Jackdaw, Goldeneye, Goosander
Open	Robin, Spotted Flycatcher

TAWNY OWL

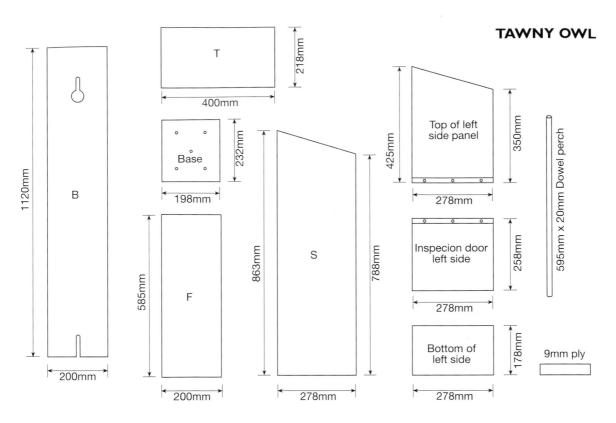

- T — 400mm × 218mm
- Base — 198mm × 232mm
- B — 1120mm × 200mm
- F — 585mm × 200mm
- S — 863mm / 788mm × 278mm
- Top of left side panel — 425mm / 350mm × 278mm
- Inspecion door left side — 258mm × 278mm
- Bottom of left side — 178mm × 278mm
- 595mm × 20mm Dowel perch
- 9mm ply

TREECREEPER

SWIFT

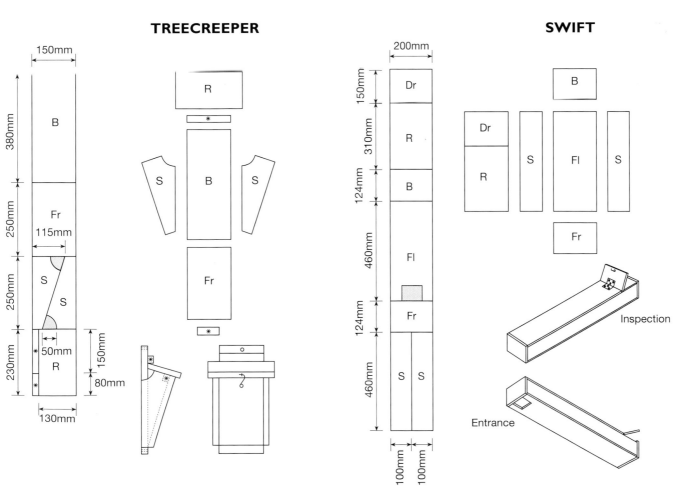

Treecreeper dimensions:
- 150mm
- B — 380mm
- Fr — 250mm, 115mm
- S — 250mm
- R — 230mm, 50mm
- 130mm
- 150mm
- 80mm

Swift dimensions:
- 200mm
- Dr — 150mm
- R — 310mm
- B — 124mm
- Fl — 460mm
- Fr — 124mm
- S S — 460mm
- 100mm, 100mm

Inspection

Entrance

ROBINS

Every time you open an envelope wishing you a Merry Christmas there is a thirty-five percent chance that a big-breasted bird is there to endorse the gesture. Big, red, cherubic, cheerful and smiling – not quite like the real thing, for robins are not always endowed with such a friendly demeanour.

A woodland species, robins have side-stepped into suburbia with comfortable alacrity and flown into favour with romantic gardeners and bird lovers alike. Of course, they'll sit on your spade as it rests in an idyllic vegetable patch whilst you treat them to a few worms and instruct them to rid your produce of pests. Yes, they'll set up home in an old kettle, a hat, a bicycle basket, paint pot or some other amusing or decorative spot, and yes if you go looking on a Christmas morning they'll have a red breast to remind you of the blood of Christ. But if you take a closer look in spring you'll see the same loveable sweeties beating nine bells out of one another. Robins are fiercely territorial and males can be excited enough to attack anything red if it appears in the wrong place. They'll quite literally peck and claw it to pieces in a flurry of shrieking and squawking – quite good fun if you're into gladiatorial baiting with birds! A stuffed robin makes an ideal decoy but a red feather or even a twist of red tissue can get one of the most aggravated specimens going.

But hey! We like robins because they like us, and yes they are often very confiding, allowing close approach and even with patience coming to the hand to feed on tasty titbits with mealworms being an ideal treat. This habit however is largely confined to the UK race, as on mainland Europe they usually shun any human association and are far more shy and skulking. Strangely they are also extremely sensitive when they begin nesting and will readily desert the nest if you disturb them too early in the egg laying process. I was sadly reminded of this last spring when allowing my four year old a squint into a nestbox at home. For this reason, site your boxes or kettles

Above: *'Oi, you lookin at me?' Robins belong to the hooligan element, always looking for a scrap – or for a few that you throw out.*

with caution and privacy. Of course it is nice to watch the adults delivering beakfuls of goodies to their brood, but if you are going to enjoy this spectacle, the predators will almost certainly be exploiting it. If you think you have hidden it well enough – hide it twice as well.

Estimates for our British population range between one and five million pairs, but they are always checked by a hard winter and of course by cats who too easily prey upon their cheeky, forgiving nature. A ripe old age for a robin, if it's able to escape the jaws and claws, might be between eight and ten years.

In the spring and summer robins feed principally on invertebrates. Almost anything of the right size can be on the menu, from ants, beetles, spiders, millipedes, slugs and snails – even small fish and lizards. In winter they'll

turn their attention to fruit and again almost anything goes - bramble, elder, rowan, spindle, buckthorn and yew to name but a few! Throughout the year they'll come to bird tables to scavenge the peanut and sunflower seed crumbs or any other minor morsels overlooked by the more specialist species. In lab tests, however, birds fed on fruit alone lost weight and died. So if it gets cold and you love your robins, splash out on some mealworms - just three grams a day is enough to keep them going through the winter.

Robins will choose almost any kind of hollow to site their nest, a bulky structure of dead leaves topped with a grassy cup lined with finer materials such as hair and very occasionally feathers. Between four and six eggs are laid and these are incubated for about two weeks by the female alone. Males return to help feed the young, which fledge after a further two weeks and are independent within a month. The youngsters' tanned, scalloped, brown plumage is exchanged for the classic red breast within three months, and by the spring they are ready for a bit of 'argie bargie' and 'how's your father' if they can find a vacant territory.

The real bonus of a robin residing in your garden is its song. A bittersweet melody, a warble with a few shrill notes. Males deliver it typically loudly in all months bar July and in winter the females chip in too. They are famed for singing under street lamps, or at night and on cold evenings it's always welcome as you dash to the warmth of

Left: The scalloped plumage of the fledgling robin has evolved for camouflage.

your door to hear a burst of such cheer.

If you've got robins, try to look after them. They are not on the slide yet, but who knows what's around the corner. Often there's a cat lurking, so make sure your scraps are placed well away from cover to give these ground feeders a chance of escaping the hidden pounce of death. If it gets tough in winter – persistent cold or prolonged ice and snow – then shop for emergency rations of mealworms to boost their diet. Hide nestboxes very well and again think cat, think mischief, think safety. Don't bother with too many boxes – unless your garden is very large, it's unlikely that a pair will tolerate another pair nesting so close, so concentrate instead on appropriate siting rather than numbers. If your offer isn't taken up in the first year, move the box – re-advertising it around Christmastime, because these little red breasted charmers are pre-occupied with fighting for your attention on the doormat before they get down to the serious springtime business of fighting for a nest site in the garden.

Below: Small, secretive and skulking, a contender for Britain's least sexy bird? Yes, until it starts to sing, because the Dunnock is a sweeter songster still and has similar requirements to the Robin – peace and catless quiet.

FIVE FAVOURITE FINCHES

I'm not so much a tit man as a finch fancier. You see finches are less fidgety, they'll actually sit still and allow you more than a quick flash of their fashionable colours. There are ten resident British species of these small, primarily seed-eating birds. While Linnets, Twite, Redpolls, Crossbills and Hawfinches should only be considered as garden rarities, there are five members of the group which you should be able to attract if you and your neighbours have a few mature shrubs or trees in the garden.

The somewhat everyday **Chaffinch** is the most numerous British finch throughout the year and it breeds country-wide. From April onwards, it builds a charming little moss-covered nest holding up to five pink eggs. The male is brightly coloured and the female drabber, both easily distinguished by their olive-green rumps and very conspicuous double white wing bars. A monotonous 'pink' call is also diagnostic. In winter our native population is swollen by an influx of visitors from Scandinavia and Northern Europe and it's then that they'll be most apparent. Chaffinches very rarely land on seed feeders and never on the nuts. Instead they are content to hop around on the ground beneath feeding stations, picking up the crumbs that fall from above. They'll eat almost anything from bread and biscuit upwards, but relish commercial ground seed mixes, which if you have a large flock are well worth supplying, and, of course, if you're lucky you may find a Brambling among them. These winter migrants always appear washed out and have a conspicuous white rump.

The next finch up the ladder will sit and hog the ports of some seed feeders all day. They're the stout, greedy, bolshy and big-billed **Greenfinches** and they'll arrive in pairs, families or small flocks. The males are fairly splendid in their yellow-green finery and the flashing yellow markings on their wings and tail are really conspicuous when they fly away. Again widespread in Britain, Greenfinches like to perch high up to sing and scan about so they too prefer fairly mature shrubberies. If you hear their twittering song with its terminal drawn-out 'swee' you will have little trouble coaxing them down to a seed feeder loaded with black sunflower seeds. They go mad for them and will clean you out repeatedly. They'll also produce a huge dirty pile of the husks, which should be swept up immediately before they begin to meld into a horrible stinking slime. Our balcony is currently flooded with this noxious mess as our Greenfinches still prefer 'husks on' to the far easier for them, and cleaner for us, sunflower hearts. Choosy, eh?

Often a pair of **Goldfinches** will arrive in winter and stay until April before they disappear to breed. Wasteland, rough grassland or roadsides are their favoured 'native' habitats where thistle, groundsel, dandelion, dock and a host of similar seeds secure their favour. These birds are pretty special. Gaudy admittedly, but dainty too, and I'm always pleased to see their red, white and black faces peering at me through the kitchen window. Nyjer seed is the key to their hearts, although sunflowers come a close second. If you have the space then plant a few teasels each year and these birds will delight in perching on top of each of the prickly, egg-shaped seed heads and helping themselves to the kernels. When all the teasel seeds have gone you can always reload the heads with sunflowers by simply pushing them into the bracts. This might well give you a great photo opportunity too.

Left: Bullfinches! A Top Ten British bird and no doubt about it. Let's hope that our remaining residents copy the continentals and start visiting feeders in earnest. And Croydon, Manchester and Wigan!

Left: *A bit flash – the chronically overcoloured Goldfinch. Who says we don't have natural exotics!*

Above: *Siskins in typical aerobatic antics on Alder, they'll also rampage through suburbia often in flocks of a hundred or more. All you need is seeds.*

I was twelve or thirteen I cycled around the neighbourhood and found no fewer than four Bullfinch nests. Today. I've yet to see or hear one in our garden and have not glimpsed that glowing white rump disappearing into cover for many months. The decline in Bullfinches has been dramatic and sad because they are simply stunning. Plump and neckless they might be but the male's pink breast almost fluoresces and contrasts marvellously with his velvety black cap. The female, who's never far away, is almost as nice with her mauvy-brown chest and each has a short stubby bill strong enough to split sloe stones and nibble through buds and seeds of many kinds. On the mainland of Europe where they are generally commoner, Bullfinches have been visiting bird tables for years but this is a habit which is only now beginning to be seen in the UK. Sunflower seeds loose on the table, but also on less busy feeders, seem to attract them but it's something I've yet to witness myself.

With the exception of Chaffinches, all these species like to nest in thick cover. Goldfinches and occasionally Greenfinches even choose the enveloping darkness of ornamental Cyprus trees, so Hawthorns, Beech, Elder or Privet are on the long-term planting list. Keep the bush dense, as it will restrict access to predators such as cats and Magpies. Planting natural food-bearing bushes is also a fairly long-term option but you could sow a border with sunflowers, teasel and thistles and edge it with some honesty. In winter all of these species have seed heads which would attract finches but I'm afraid that two or three stems of each may not be enough to pull the birds in. Finches like fields so think as big as you can!

Left: *Bickering on the bag – male Siskins get possessive over peanuts but it's not this which leads them to see red. They seem to have a genuine fondness for the colour itself.*

Siskins are very small finches, distinctively yellow, green and black in colour with a deeply forked tail and squeaking 'tsy-zii' call. You'll be fortunate to be visited in summer but in winter, when their numbers can often be greatly increased by overseas visitors, they are fairly regular feeders in large or more open gardens. Siskins are highly acrobatic and will swarm onto seed and nut dispensers and show a definite preference for those with red fittings. This became apparent years ago when retailers began offering peanuts in orange-red plastic ready to hang bags. They still do, so if you fancy trying for Siskins start with a couple of these, but take care, it requires less than a nano-second for squirrels to bite open the bags and shed their load to the ground, and these flighty little birds won't go for them down there.

At the pinnacle of the British finch list is the wonderful **Bullfinch**. One night after school when

BLACKBIRDS
BUSKING BEAUTIES ARE TOP OF THE POPS

The day decays into a deep purple and the street lights switch to red and then glow through to orange. As the chill sets in from the clear sky and televisions flicker inside rooms waiting for tea-time, the virtuoso takes his stand on the silhouetted aerial. A fluent symphony of beautiful flutey notes is warbled in a liquid contralto, which lasts only eight or ten seconds, but is repeated gloriously several times in a minute. The Blackbird is the supreme suburban songster, blowing the Robin or the late-lamented Song Thrush clean out of the avian charts. And Blackbirds are newcomers; during the nineteenth century they were solitary and elusive birds of dense thickets, much as they are today in parts of mainland Europe. It was only really after the First World War that they shed their shy and retiring habits and stormed into suburbia.

Our humble Blackbird occupies most of Europe, North Africa and a band that stretches from Turkey to China. Britain's Blackbirds are sedentary but in winter are joined by continentals, many of which continue down to central Spain. In most parts of the UK they will be the commonest breeding species in gardens, and their rough grass nests can be hidden almost anywhere, from a cleft in an apple tree, to a roll of wire behind the shed. The substantial cup holds up to six eggs from March onwards, although clutches can be found in any month of the year. The female alone incubates for two weeks and the young fledge in another two. In two more she starts all over again. In the meantime all the males in the area will be at war; they strike mad postures when disputing territories, fanning tails, stretching necks and puffing themselves up, even fighting – not quite to the death!

Blackbirds are true omnivores, and having the biggest bill of all our resident thrushes, they focus upon the larger items in each class of food. Earthworms are fundamentally important to their ecology, and their head cocked, peering-down-and-listening posture, followed by a hop-see-swallow can be seen on lawns country-wide.

Left: *Stunning! Male Blackbird with a beak to die for. Which savages still put these in pies? Show me the whites of their eyes!*

A huge diversity of invertebrate prey is consumed and an even greater variety of fruits, berries and seeds. Yew, holly, hawthorn, rowan, apple and elder are favourites, but they'll gobble up whatever's there.

Consequently, catering for Blackbirds couldn't be easier – offer whatever you've got in the way of fruits and dry scraps. Maintain a well aerated and drained lawn to provide an earthworm supply, and ban insecticides. When it comes to planting food-bearing bushes, yew is an impossibly slow-growing species and holly not very speedy either. Go for rowan and especially elder, which produces huge flower heads that attract loads of insects, and lots of berries to satisfy all tastes. It also produces good nesting cover before it reaches maturity and 'opens-up' inside. Ivy is good for nest sites too and should be allowed to riot along a fence or a wall. For years we had such a resource in my parents' cat-ridden garden but no nests. As soon as a dog was taken in, several successful Blackbird broods a year were fledged, a fact that has always suggested to me that Blackbirds are keen on secrecy and security when it comes to breeding.

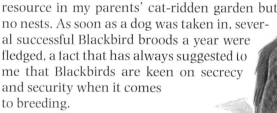

Left: A *speckly juvenile gobbles rowan berries.* Right: *Here a pair get to grips with elderberries, another favourite on the menu.*

SONG THRUSHES

A late snow had fallen one April and I slipped and skidded on my Clark's shiny soles all the way to the school grounds where two Song Thrush nests were hidden in a tangle of elder and old man's beard. The birds slipped silently away as I crept through the caves beneath the bushes. What they left on that crisp Saturday I shall never forget. A bowl of pale brown, perfectly smooth mud, ringed with grass, and lying in this archetypal nest were five sky-blue eggs each dotted with purple, almost black, spots. The other held two miniature 'freak eggs', each the size of a Malteser, but still perfectly marked.

Song Thrushes were never as visibly common as Blackbirds but it was a rarity if, in any spring and summer, I pushed my bike back into its shed without having being stirred by just such a sight. In fact I became complacent, writing only 'S.T' in my nature note books. Had I only known what was to come! Now it's at least three years since I last pulled myself into a hedge and glimpsed that little cameo. Our thrushes are on the brink.

Let's not pretend we don't know why – our farmland is a rolled expanse of chemically ravaged wilderness and our gardens are pest-free plots where we are obsessed with tidiness. Okay, that may sound confrontational, but you get my point.

Like Blackbirds, Song Thrushes are principally dependent upon earthworms to shore up their diet. It is only when worms are in short supply that they turn to snails, the prey to which they have become inextricably linked owing to their habit of bashing them against stones to access the soft body of the animal. Song Thrushes are also less cosmopolitan in their choice of vegetable matter, it seems that being able to turn to snails is the way they typically survive. So it's in our hands, probably literally. Dump the slug pellets safely in the bin and accept a few holes in your prized green-stuffs and your local Song Thrushes might make it, but if we continue to effect a 'molluscan

Right: Unfortunately the French eat both, which doesn't help when a species is in decline.

Right and below: *Rich and varied is the song - a great start to an early day in suburbia.*

genocide' across suburbia, it might be that the last snail becomes the last straw.

Branch Bundles and Stick Piles

Years ago, I remember reading in a pamphlet about gardening for wildlife that if you were short of bushes, you might encourage birds to nest in your garden by suspending loose bundles of branches on your walls and fences. Because I could imagine nothing but a few sparrows sitting in them and thought that it would look ridiculous I dismissed this as an 'armchair' idea and forgot about it. But during the autumn before last we felled a willow and a storm-blown birch in the garden, and piled all of the brash at the base of a dead oak trunk. By spring a pair of Robins had taken up residence in the impenetrable tangle. Then a Dunnock joined in, then a Blackbird and then the Robins again and then the Dunnocks again! Five successful broods flew out of our huge heap of branches! So now it's going to stay. I've had to promise to move it and 'house' it more neatly behind a fence in the corner. If you have the space, why not give it a go?

GREAT SPOTTED WOODPECKERS
ENOUGH TO MAKE YOU ANTHROPOMORPHIC

Few creatures are so cartoon, so much caricatures of themselves and so basically exciting as woodpeckers. They are essentially funny; anything that regularly hammers its head against hard wood is bound to carry the burden of humour. And 'Greater Spots' are naughty too, always looking over their shoulders expecting a telling off for nothing more than going about their rather mad business. They're brightly marked and brash, with a laugh fit for a dockside tavern at closing time. It's true, and once in a while there's nothing wrong with anthropomorphism!

Although these birds prefer stands of timber with more than a few mature trees, using hedgerows, railway embankments, copses and parklands, they are able to penetrate deep into urban environments. You're unlikely to mistake their striking pied plumage or red undertail coverts or their harsh and far-carrying 'tchack' call. But drumming is best. In spring, males advertise their territories by striking an appropriately resonant branch rapidly and repeatedly with their beak. A short but powerful burst of sonic fire results and no doubt excites the females. The nesting hole is excavated in trunks or branches and a chamber holds up to six eggs which both parents incubate for just over two weeks. The appallingly ugly young emerge about three weeks later and proceed to make a horrendous din for the rest of the summer.

Great Spotted Woodpeckers have relatively short, stout beaks with squared-off chisel-shaped tips and use these to both hammer and prise apart dead wood in pursuit of grubs and bugs. Fruit, seeds and nuts are also on the menu, as are the nestlings of other birds and often they will either cunningly catch them inside their nest boxes, by pretending to be their parents outside, or by battering a hole through the front of the box. The luckless fledglings are dragged out and be pecked to bits on a nearby branch. Nature raw, in beak and claw! Fortunately, you can tempt them with less bloodthirsty bait - fat, suet and peanuts, particularly in winter when it's not so necessary to focus on a protein-rich diet to

Left: *Remember when Woody was still a woodpecker? With some of these guys on your feeder you won't need animated astronauts to help the story along.*

rear their young. If you make 'birdcakes' from fat mixes and hang them up you may encounter a couple of problems. Firstly, other birds, especially Starlings, also love them and will steal most of your woodpecker's food before these slightly shyer birds can take advantage of it. Secondly, once familiarized, the 'peckers themselves will soon learn to sever the string and send the whole thing tumbling to the ground where it's easier for them to eat it but also easier for rats to discover it, you to tread in it, and worst of all, miss all of the action. An alternative design to suit primarily 'peckers is to take a heavy log complete with bark and drill or cut holes in it, say 2 cm diameter and 3 cm deep, at regular intervals along its length. Then plug these with your fat mixture while it's still malleable and hang or stand it in position. It won't prove exclusive but it's slightly more natural and as such, might, if you've chosen creatively, offer a photographic opportunity. If you become a major fan of *Dendrocopos major* then treat them by including mealworms in your fat mix. They'll love you, albeit anthropomorphically!

Above: *The sexes are separable. Males have a crimson nape – something that is only really conspicuous when they are at rest.*

THREE TREATS!
TWO NUTTERS AND SOME FAT FELLOWS

Nuthatch

My friend Ian says that Nuthatches look 'hard' but I think they simply lack any sense of humour or for that matter many social graces. I am sorry to anthropomorphize again but it's true. They bark their snappy and aggressive calls to each other with little decorum and seem to consistently bear grudges, posturing and bickering over a few old nuts.

Casting such notions aside, Nuthatches are almost mini woodpeckers, equipped with large, dagger-shaped bills. They climb the bark with similar alacrity but focus instead on gleaning insects from the surface or from cracks, and feed on smaller seeds such as beechmast and soft hazelnuts. These they wedge into crevasses in trees or walls before they hammer them apart to peck out the kernels. They'll do the same to any loose peanuts you provide as they loathe spending any time away from the security of the tree trunk when feeding. They'll hang on to nut feeders for sure, but seem to resent it and invariably upset all the other birds, so I feed them with a separate pile of their own loose peanuts. If you have any local, mature or even old oak, beech or hazel woodland you should try for them. Tolerate their anti-social antics and should they deign to nest in your garden you will witness a work of great artistry as they neatly plaster up the entrance to any cavity with mud until precisely the diameter they favour is achieved. Curiously, when using nest boxes they'll also cement around the lid from inside – mad, eh?!

Jay

Another woodlander that might sneak into your garden is the exotic-looking Jay. Jays will stealthily approach bird tables loaded with loose food, particularly peanuts, and then only land for as long as it take to stuff up their especially large throat sacks. Typically, this adaptation is used to carry up to nine acorns, which they hoard in their private larders. Exceptionally they'll secrete these up to two miles away and being crows, and thus among the most 'intelligent' of birds they actually remember where the large majority are hidden. Of course, those that they forget germinate and may go on to become trees. Jays are probably the most important method by which oaks spread uphill. Trivial Pursuit – my middle name!

Woodpigeon

Okay, I know, you're thinking 'Three Treats' Nuthatch, Jay and... Woodpigeon! What the...? But look, what else do you get in your garden that isn't covered somewhere in this book? I mean, yes, Treecreepers, Hawfinches and Woodcock are interesting birds, but not regular in most gardens. So let's get real and enjoy what we've got: Woodpigeons.

I once read somewhere that the damage to crops, combined with the size of their population, made Woodpigeons the most serious bird pests in Britain. Apparently they cause more than a million pounds worth of damage to clover, brassicas, lettuce and peas. Can you tell me how much damage we do to the environment each year and quantify it in pounds sterling? In my garden 'Woodies' are welcome. They come to feed on acorns and recently I spied no fewer than sixteen on the lawn. When the acorns run out I shall feed them a cheap cereal-based ground food mix and if one nests in one of our trees I shall enjoy its gentle and therapeutic cooing.

THE TRUTH ABOUT SPARROWHAWKS AND MAGPIES

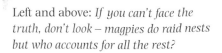

It's sad but true, that like a lovelorn soldier I carry a small collection of photographs in my wallet. I'm away from home a lot and it's good to put a favourite face to a crackling voice on a satellite phone. But sandwiched between my girlfriend, little girl, a Ferrari 246 GT Dino, Audrey Hepburn on a bicycle and Stirling Moss's autographed business card is a flimsy picture of a male **Sparrowhawk** cut from a magazine. He stares with fixed fury, his chrome yellow eyes blazing over his burnished blue back, his trousers fluffing over his lengthy legs, standing in a puddle reflecting the neat barring on his breast. When it comes to loved ones, pin-ups, fantasies and heroes he scores in all four categories – for me at least, the best bird in Britain and a contender for the world title. Sparrowhawks tease us with their jet fighter fly-bys, their flashes of dun shadow going away in silence through the wood. They tantalise us by leaving fresh kills on the footpath, the flesh still warm, the feathers still floating on the wind, or with their delicate whinneying call, close behind a cloak of birch rendering them invisible. Sparrowhawks – you've always just missed them.

Above: *If you can't face the truth, don't look – death is essential to all life*

But now after years of waiting we are all in with a chance. After more than a century of senseless persecution by gamekeepers and two decades of pesticide poisoning, the population of these dainty little raptors lay in ruins. In many parts they were a rarity or absent altogether, but gradually over the last thirty years they have spread back to their old haunts and into a few new neighbourhoods too. And because so many of the farmland refugees have concentrated in our gardens then so have their predators. In many places Sparrowhawks have joined Kestrels as an urban species. Who can blame them? All that food, buzzing around feeders and on tables, rearing broods in boxes, is a veritable bonanza!

I hope that most of us enjoy the Sparrowhawk's brief visits; some people even get great views occasionally. That Sparrowhawks snatch a few Tits is, of course, perfectly natural, and we should be no less disturbed than when we watch a fly struggling in a spider's web. Predation makes the natural world and your garden go round. Thus it saddens me to read in magazines, or to receive mail from those who hate these raiders, who want them 'controlled', who blame them for falling songbird numbers. Look, they had a tough time, you forgot you existed, now you feed the birds and by so doing so you feed them. This is nature, it's self-regulating, if there weren't enough small birds in your garden there wouldn't be any Sparrowhawks. They'd produce less young, stop breeding altogether, or fly off somewhere else. If Nightingales enjoyed a similarly remarkable recovery would you complain that they kept you awake at night? Probably. Get a life, and stop letting your human emotions get in the way of good biology!

This brings us neatly from the raider to the bandit, the burglar, the vandal, the current all-round-bad guy of the bird world: the wonderful **Magpie**!

If I had a pound for every gripe I've heard about the mischievous murdering Magpie I wouldn't be writing this book, I'd be looking for Shoe-billed Storks in a swamp in Uganda. Magpies have become complete scapegoats, if a bird can be anything to do with a goat, and are widely, and sadly seriously, believed to be responsible for the dramatic decline in songbird numbers, particularly in suburbia. Let's get a few things straight.

Magpies are adept at raiding birds' nests and eating, either the eggs, or the young. They do not often kill adult birds. Thus they exert their impact on small bird populations from late March through to June, for perhaps three or three and a half months of the year. The eggs and young are not part of the all-important breeding base of any species population, and are thus less important in the potential recruitment of new individuals.

Left and above: *If you can't face the truth, don't look – magpies do raid nests but who accounts for all the rest?*

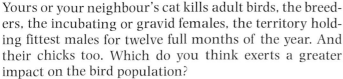

Above: *Noisy and obvious, like American G.I.s sixty years ago, magpies beg for trouble.*

Left: *Oh yes! Even Audrey Hepburn struggles against beauties like this enduring favourite.*

And don't forget that Magpies are omnivores, that will scavenge anything at some times of the year. They're not strict carnivores that must have meat. Ask yourself, when was the last time you saw a cat eating a salad?

Yes, Magpies have increased; they've tripled their numbers in the last twenty years, probably because of a relaxation in persecution, although we've yet to understand all the nuances that have allowed them to expand their niche so quickly. But it must have occurred in response to something, a new or changed opportunity. So it's strange therefore that the Magpie started to expand pretty much when the really dramatic decline started to occur in farmland bird populations. Ask yourself, which animal do you know that increases its numbers when there's less of its 'food' available, and continues to do so until there is nearly no 'food' left? Perhaps small birds are not its 'food' at all, or at least not the part of its diet that influences its own population changes. It seems likely that the increase and decline are not linked, and thankfully both the RSPB and BTO agree with me.

Yours or your neighbour's cat kills adult birds, the breeders, the incubating or gravid females, the territory holding fittest males for twelve full months of the year. And their chicks too. Which do you think exerts a greater impact on the bird population?

Next up. Magpies are bluey green, black and white, noisy birds with long tails. They sit on tree tops, roofs, and readily fly across roads in front of cars. They are highly apparent in the environment. Dunnocks on the other hand are dowdy little brown birds which skulk like mice beneath bushes and are relatively timid, even in suburbia. Ask yourself, do I see more magpies than I see Dunnocks, and does that mean there are really more Magpies than Dunnocks where I live? You see, drive by, or walking to the paper-shop bird censusing techniques are not without their flaws.

A study of twenty-three songbird species using data collected since 1962 and published in 1998 showed no correlation between the relative increases in Sparrowhawks and Magpies and decreases in smaller birds. Indeed, in some areas songbirds thrived in spite of the increased predator numbers. The most respected and informed juries have considered the accusations. Result – Not Guilty. Case Closed.

BIRDS ON CAMERA
DO-IT-YOURSELF WILDLIFE TELEVISION

There are a couple of recent inventions which have helped our garden birds into the video age. Spurred on by the enormous success of Bill Oddie's and Peter Holden's '*Bird in the Nest*' series on BBC TV, and enabled by the rise in quality and decline in cost of small security type video cameras, a number of companies offer a neat package which allows you to witness all the shenanigans that unfold as a brood of birds, typically Blue Tits, are reared in a nest box. Their standard kit comes complete with a nest box, some with a choice of Blue Tit or Great Tit sized entrance hole, a tiny infra-red camera and a ten to twenty metre lead which runs into your television, video or computer.

The cameras are normally fixed focus, but of a sufficiently wide angle that everything is sharp from the entrance hole down to the bottom of the nest cup. The image is black and white but surprisingly good; though because the camera is placed in the roof of the box one limitation is the single top view which sometimes means you get a lot of chicks' crowns and not much else. The benefit is that the lens remains relatively clean through the early stages of the brood stay. As they begin to get

Left: Take One – fresh from 'costume' and 'make-up', a Great Tit poses nicely for a repositioned camera. Less privacy than Hello Magazine!

'feathered up' the lens gets pretty dusty and may need cleaning. In the three that I have investigated this is quick and easy and shouldn't disturb the birds too much, as it is facilitated by unclipping and raising the hinged lid, removing the camera from its socket, wiping and replacing it, something that can be done in two minutes or less. Note that this also means that there is no need to leave the camera in the box when it's not in use. When you are sure the birds have settled, preferably when the clutch is complete or even after hatching, you can quickly slip the camera in and begin viewing. Some even have a microphone so you don't miss out on any of the squeaking. It's never quite *Wildlife on One*, but they are your birds, there's never a shortage of activity and on this account the show is particularly enjoyed by children.

At least one of the manufacturers offers an alternative box suitable for Starlings, which I can only imagine would be as much fun as tits. The starter kits cost around two hundred pounds and they get my vote because although that's a big outlay for fourteen days of bird-watching a year, they reveal a little bit of secret bird life that you never otherwise see.

Also on offer are bird boxes where the camera is pointing out of the hole, or bird tables with a similarly hidden device. The former you site in range of your feeding facilities, the latter you erect, load with food, connect up and sit back to watch. These cameras supply colour images and to be honest they suffer in strong sunlight. as the currently available cheaper video cameras fail to deal with contrast as well. Often under such conditions the subject is dark and the background washed out. Of course you can maximise the quality by repositioning the set-up to reduce the difference in relative lighting intensity, but they never quite make it, providing as they do merely a close-up of something you can see more clearly through your binoculars or telescope.

Recently I have invested in a wireless CCD security system. This consists of a colour digital camera about the

Above: *Take Two – top view of the finished clutch, the ideal time to introduce the camera, thus minimising disturbance.*

Above: *Take Three – action! Here comes the caterpillar, and the fledgling Blue Tits are clamouring for more.*

size of a chunky TV remote controller fitted with a wide angle lens. A flap on top folds up and can be angled to transmit via microwave the image and sound over a distance of three hundred metres to the receiver, which sits on top of the television or video. This means it can be used anywhere in the garden without any cabling. It simply screws on top of a normal camera tripod and you can site it at will, preferably with a reasonably clear line of sight to the receiver, glass not reducing the quality of reception. The pictures are excellent; they suffer in strong sunlight, but in low light and with a black and white camera they come into their own. Two little rows of infra-red LRDs either side of the lens seem to throw out enough light to produce quite acceptable images in near darkness.

The camera is not water or squirrel proof so I intend to make up a metal box to house it, then I'll feel more confident about leaving it outside in all weathers and in all positions. The wireless benefits are obvious; it's quick and easy to move. In one quite expensive swoop most of

the diurnal and nocturnal wildlife in the garden is on Channel Six in the kitchen, and if I don't feel like waiting up I stick in a three-hour tape and simply rewind for the action in the morning, all the while perfecting my David Attenborough impersonation!

Recently I had the good fortune of visiting Graham Roberts at his home in Havant, Hampshire. He had cannibalised a Blue Tit camera box to sneak unique views of a pair of swifts that were nesting in his loft. He showed me some fascinating tape of the birds' nesting process including delicate mutual preening, egg turning, the constant addition of feathers to the unsubstantial nest and the sleeping adults cuddling all night. One regularly puts its young over the other's back in an embrace. Graham's genius for getting 'into' nests knows few bounds, he's done the same for Peregrines too and the pictures are great. Anyone for Treecreepers?

MAMMALS

FOXES
A FEW HOME TRUTHS

Above and below: *Not just a pretty face. Radar-dish ears – all the better to hear you with – a nose to die for and eyes that can see in near darkness. Simply beautiful evolution.*

He is neither cunning nor crafty, nor even very quick or brown. He has never killed indiscriminately or wantonly and I'd put a pound on the fact that he's never harmed a cat. Okay, he used to pull your dustbin over before the introduction of the wildlife unfriendly wheelie bin, and yes, he'll dig up lawns and flowerbeds and even the shallow graves of your late beloved hamsters. Okay, he'll leave his bitter scent on your trees and clusters of faeces in prominent places and in the winter time his mate will let out a blood curdling cough and scream throughout the night. If you're lucky, you might live in a neighbourhood where every day you are afforded views of one of the most attractive characters in our fauna, the Red Fox.

In low, late autumn sun when foxes have grown their winter coats, to see one anywhere, let alone in your garden is a very special treat. They are exquisitely marked on the head and face and too perfectly proportioned to qualify for the 'pretty' tag. They are simply beautiful.

I've had my property damaged by foxes – in fact *I've* been damaged by foxes and still have the scars to prove it. I used to keep them as a boy, but despite bloody set backs and ripped and chewed clothes they remain a very firm favourite. The fox is a creature that comes to us young but always with baggage – generally a poor representation based on equally poor biology. For instance; foxes will break in to somebody's chicken run and go mad killing all the chickens. To the fox the hen-house is a supermarket and when you visit the human version do you only come home with enough food for one meal? No, and nor would the fox if, as under natural conditions, it were allowed to repeatedly return to the shop each night to pick up another ready to eat fowl. This isn't a psychopathic animal – it's an efficient shopper! And this is the twenty-first century, if smallholders and farmers alike will not implement the incredibly cheap and effective means of fox proofing their poultry, then *vive le fox*!

Foxes are omnivores and will turn their noses up at very little you might offer. Ours get kitchen scraps of all kinds and the occasional meat treats. They are not perturbed by oriental fare or by hot curries, but to date have not acquired a taste for prawn crackers! We feed all year round and I have no doubt that this is of some dietary use to our foxes, particularly in the winter and spring when reduced foraging time and care of their cubs are considerations. I've spent many evenings watching foxes, badgers and cats together in gardens. There is a clear hierarchy; foxes are at the bottom of the pecking order with cats very securely at the top – if they want to be. Many cats are curious about these visitors but unless there are any titbits they fancy for themselves they don't bother to get involved. If fresh chicken is on the menu then your cuddly Tibbles easily chases off Reynard and Brock with a bit of hissing and hackle raising. Thus true stories of cats as fox prey I would say are largely unfounded, if not extremely rare.

LIVING WITH URBAN FOXES

Trevor Williams's uncle had a farm. He didn't really like foxes but he reckoned the hunt did more damage than they were worth, and that it wasn't worth giving up one day to chase one fox because it had pinched one chicken. 'Nature's burglars' he called them, and young Trevor fell for their mischievous charms and has never fallen for another. Nine years ago he started the Fox Project in Tonbridge in Kent, and now each year sees him caring and rehabilitating hundreds of injured adults and abandoned fox cubs. He employs four part-time staff and is helped by a team of ninety volunteers. Paradoxically, the other side of the charity is concerned with people who don't like foxes, or don't want anything to do with them. When it comes to knowing what the public think about foxes I figure Trevor knows best, so I asked him a few questions.

Left: Watching four cubs at play is not only entertaining but an insight into how they'll behave as adults. They sniff, stalk and pounce, and it gets rougher and rougher.

Question: So what don't people like about foxes?
Answer: Well, it's all sorts, everything from noise, particularly in January when they are beginning to mate, through to fear of them attacking their pets. If it's the noise, we tell them to just close their windows and turn up the stereo – even if they succeed in chasing the fox from their property, they'll hear it from next door! There's not much you can do about noise.

Question: And the pet issue, that's nonsense too. isn't it?
Answer: Yes and no. I know of one attack on a dog, a Jack Russell that was trying to get at a den with cubs. The vixen bit him on the nose. As for cats, I have no personal evidence of foxes ever killing cats, but I've heard of a half a dozen cases which I might give some credence to, probably a result of the cats again harrying fox cubs. If people complain about rabbits and guinea pigs going missing then we say, 'They're natural prey – house them properly and they'll be totally safe'.

Question: What about garden damage – digging, etc.
Answer: We get hundreds of calls about this, in fact we run a taped advice line. Basically it's about deterrents. The problems are nuisance damage, such as digging holes, scent marking, which many people find offensive, and territorial

Left: 'Get lost vole-breath, I've got a head-ache' – or a moment of tenderness between a pair of suburban beauties.

marking with faeces. Not surprisingly, people object to having their lawns covered in fox pooh and they can also worry about health and hygiene problems, the *Toxocara* parasite that can cause blindness in children. Firstly, we tell people to pick it up, pooper scoop it, and then if the faeces are on grass we recommend using a product called 'Scoot'. Used as directed, this works; rather than get caught out foxes just stay away. If the mess is on soil or concrete then we recommend using 'Renardine', which if you decant onto a small pile of sharp-sand will stay active longer and not drain away into the ground. Planter Bags also seem to be favourite sites for this sort of action. Try 'Get-my-garden' here – it's safe, based on citronella, but its jelly pellets don't last as long as the others. Lastly, we always suggest that repellants are placed where the animal can be found

left: *When very young, fox cubs are more 'kitten' than 'puppy' but they already have that distinctive odour as Trevor betrays here!*

dripped on. You've got to persevere and it's slow, but it definitely works.

Question: **Dare I mention rabies?**
Answer: Well imagine the paranoia that will result when eventually a 'bona fide' case appears over here. It's going to be horrible. The disease is hugely exaggerated. Anyway, it's on the decline in Europe, there hasn't been a human fatality since 1972, and the vaccines and treatments for us are up to date.

Question: **Historically the Fox swings to and fro in favour – what's the current score?**
Answer: Lots of short-lived, loud shouting by a few people, while the vast majority secretly enjoy

entering the garden. Check for paw prints on fences, footprints, hairs. We've tried the ultrasonic deterrents, but found them only eighty two per cent effective, compared to the chemicals at ninety four. You'll never create a fox-free zone, but you can definitely reduce their activity.

them. I don't think mange or anything else has made them unpopular, people like foxes in suburbia. One day last year I skidded to a halt to get a better view of a fox in a field, then I sat there thinking, 'Hey you've got hundreds of these things in your care at home'. Once foxes have gripped you it takes more than a little nuisance to put you off.

Question: **You haven't mentioned mange?**
Answer: In the seventies we hardly saw any mange, but now it's spread almost everywhere. Bristol is the worst area, and because it is canine mange people do fear that it could spread to their pets. No one knows how easily this might happen – the research is ambiguous, it might need direct contact, or it could be windborn. It might survive in the grass. If your dog does contract mange it is easy to treat and cure and there is no reason for your pet to end up looking as scabby as some of the poor foxes.

Question: **What's the Fox Project's opinion on feeding foxes.**
Answer: We say if you want to feed them, then do it, but make sure the food is a bonus, not a new life style. Feed them two or three times a week, randomly and don't try to domesticate them. Don't feed them too close to the house, let alone indoors, and never by hand. No sloppy dog food – give them kitchen scraps.

Question: **So can we treat it ourselves?**
Answer: Yes, definitely and effectively, but never pharmeceutically. The chemicals work well in captivity where you can inject them but dripping them onto bait is too risky. They can kill other animals including pets if they steal the bait first, and besides we are having great success with a completely harmless homeopathic treatment, which is cheaper too. Arsenicum and Sulphur can be crushed from tablets and dusted onto food, or the liquid

Trevor Williams is my kind of conservationist – pragmatic, realistic, and efficient. The Fox Project offers information and advice to local authorities country-wide. It helps Environmental Health Officers, parks personnel and the public, providing up to date advice. They won't like the tag but Trevor and his team are experts. If you really need to, ring them on 01732 367 397 or the Help Line – Repellants 0906 272 4411 and Mange 0906 272 4422, 25p. per minute, tapes last four minutes.

INVERTEBRATES

THE RISE OF THE MINIBEAST

When I was four, sometimes all I needed was a matchbox with a few holes punched in the top. My mother typically used the outside tine of a table fork for this and sometimes the sweet-smelling, paper-covered pine would splinter and I'd have to wait for another box to empty. Sometimes she'd have the patience to swop all the matches into the damaged carton and let me have the other. As you can tell, detail was important to me – that's because I was a young entomologist. For my fifth and maybe my best ever birthday I received the *Observers' Book of Common Insects and Spiders*. I still have it. The dustjacket is fairly intact, it smells more like a book than most books do these days, and I can still remember every illustration, even lines from the poetry that it included. Today I'd say that it appears as a charming but rather old-fashioned book, not like this one! But in the hands of a five-year-old in the year that England won the World Cup it was brilliant. You see, it was a grown-ups' insect book, a veritable treatise with diagrams and scientific names. While ladybirds continued to fascinate me, the books by the same name were consigned to the baby-book-bin, and I rose to the challenge of recognizing a *Chrysopa carnea* when I found one.

Now you may surmise that I was precocious little swot, but if that's the case, I've met lots more. Children whose single-minded interest leads them to focus in such an obsessive way that their narrow field of knowledge rivals that of many adults. That's why I don't like 'minibeasts'. It's a naff catch phrase, a dumbing down which isn't nec-essary. You don't, in my opinion, need to 'sell' ladybirds and stag beetles to children. What could sell itself better than a beautiful little red beetle with countable spots, that tickles as it runs up your finger to hesitate thrice before it wafts away like a fairy. Or than the armoured robo-crea-ture with massive horns and attitude enough to threaten giants like five-year-olds! Maybe I'm being pedantic, but I still get a bigger buzz when some kid wan-ders up and asks me what I think of his or her *Dytiscus* than when another whines on about the 'feelers' on their 'creepy-crawly'. They are antennae and it's an invertebrate and kids like know-ing more than us. Please don't offend them.

But now I must eat some humble pie, because the best book I've ever had about finding, catching and housing inverte-brates was written by Roma Oxford and published by the Yorkshire Wildlife Trust. Yorkshire Electricity very kindly sponsored it and it's called: *Minibeast Magic!* (Ouch!) It has no rival; no more serious tome, is, or could be as useful. It's wonderfully practical and resourceful. It's also delightfully illustrated. Frankly, if you or your family have an iota of interest in minibeasts (Arrgggghhh!) then get hold of this book. There, it hasn't got shiny red elytra with twin or other spots so I've given it a hard sell!

Wherever you live and whatever your garden is like, it will have hundreds, if not thousands, if not tens of thou-sands of invertebrates living in it. Insects, Spiders, Crustaceans, Molluscs, Millipedes, Centipedes, and Annelids, not to mention Protozoans, Rotifers, and

Right: 'The diversity of form and function in common inverte-brate life should provide no end of wonder for juvenile humans'.
A. J. C. Feggit, Entomologist and Sociologist (imaginary)

Nematodes. The vast majority of these life forms are microscopic and we'll all live our lives without ever seeing them or knowing their names, let alone understanding how they keep our gardens going in the great scheme of things. It's the bigger terrestrial invertebrates which we can more easily get to know or know better, and either process is fascinating because these are the creatures that could not be less human, more alien than any others on earth. Look at a snail winding up a stem, what could be more different than you in structure? Consider a beetle scuttling beneath the bark, what can it be seeing, sensing, what is its life like? And the dragonfly hanging on sparkling wings, what does it see, what does it feel as it arcs skywards to snatch a fly? You see, it's impossible but we have to try, and when we fail we must just wonder.

Compared with the birds and mammals that we love so much, there is a truly awesome diversity of invertebrate life on, under or just beyond our doorsteps. To ignore it is a waste, to harm it is ignorant, and to exterminate it dangerous. If you do one thing this summer, pull on some old jeans and a jumper, and go and lie in the garden flat out, face down and peer about until you discover a 'new' species. Play Darwin, pretend to be Attenborough, make up a name for it, call it *Fastcrawlerii smithus*. Please don't miss out on the magic of minibeasts (or invertebrates, as they really are).

Over the next few spreads this book covers just a few of these animals. Not all are 'popular', a few are much maligned, some loathed. In contrast, others are lauded and loved, celebrated in art and literature, endowed with almost spiritual significance. Whatever, they are creatures that try to live with us and therefore deserve a break.

Taking a closer look

Direct observation is always the best way of learning about the behaviour of any animal, watching from a non-intrusive distance. But this can be very difficult with small creatures, especially invertebrates; after a few seconds of manic scuttling, they disappear under a leaf or into a crevice never to be seen again. So to get to grips with the antics

Left: The perfect birthday treat – a good quality robust glass hand lens that will focus fresh eyes upon a superior detail than toyshop plastic items.

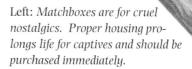

Left: Matchboxes are for cruel nostalgics. Proper housing prolongs life for captives and should be purchased immediately.

of ants, the behaviour of beetles or the habits of harvestmen, it is best to capture them and make observations over a few hours or days in a suitable vivarium. Trained, gentle and fearless fingers can be very good for carefully collecting many robust species – Stag Beetles, Cockchafers, large snails, slugs or earthworms. But others are more tricky. Have you ever tried picking up a centipede?

Pooters

Most simply a tablespoon and a soft watercolour paintbrush make a fine combination, the brush for chivvying or teasing from cracks and the spoon as the carrier. However, for fast-moving or very small animals the humble pooter is the best tool. These suction traps can be bought from entomological suppliers, or easily constructed at home.

A few simple guidelines: no ants, nothing else likes their formic acid which they will undoubtedly discharge upon pooting; no slugs, everything small gets stuck in their slime; no spiders in mixed bags, they'll eat everything else; don't overcrowd your pooter, empty it regularly, transferring by paintbrush those animals you intend to keep, and always suck gently, many creatures are fragile, and the pinging of a dizzy beetle richocheting around your pooter is not acceptable.

Many other invertebrate species are normally invisible to us so 'trapping' will increase the scope of your collecting. Dig out your partner's or parents' umbrella or better still get hold of an intact old one! Find a large stick and proceed beneath the low boughs of an oak. Hold the 'brolly upside down by its spike over your head and gen-

Above: Shop for or manufacture soft muslin nets. Cheap coarse nylon newsagent specials will soon destroy or dismember any bugs or butterflies.

tly tap the overhanging branches. A myriad bugs, beetles, caterpillars and spiders will tumble down and you can paintbrush or poot them out accordingly.

Pit-fall traps

Pit-fall traps are great for catching nocturnal species. Thoroughly clean a 2-litre clear plastic soft drinks bottle, dry it and then cut around its sides about 15-20 cm from the base and again 2 cm below the neck. Discard the middle tube, invert the top and fit it snuggly into the cup base. Staple the two together with four paper staples, bury it in the ground so that the lip is flush with the soil's surface and cover with a loose fitting piece of bark.

Check for captives at least daily and remove from the ground when not in use.

The young naturalist's favourite method of housing insects – the jam-jar – might be better known as the torture chamber. A few holes punched in its lid are not enough for adequate ventilation. Always replace with a mesh cover; a square of fabric cut from old tights held in place with an elastic band is an improvement, but a clear plastic sweet jar or a wider topped tank will be more successful in terms of climate control. Entomological suppliers provide tanks, tubs or boxes for adults and larvae of all kinds of invertebrate, so if you're serious it's worth the spend.

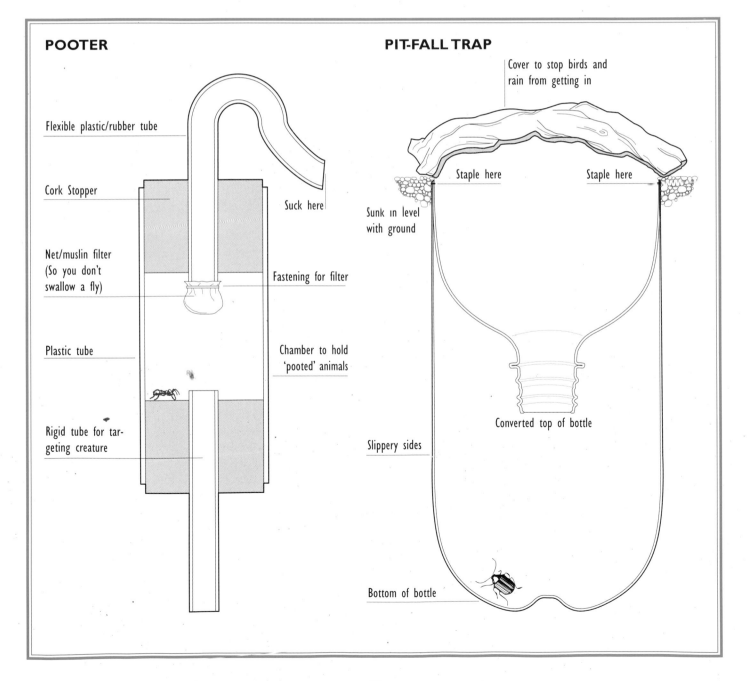

POOTER

Flexible plastic/rubber tube

Cork Stopper

Net/muslin filter
(So you don't
swallow a fly)

Plastic tube

Rigid tube for targeting creature

Suck here

Fastening for filter

Chamber to hold 'pooted' animals

PIT-FALL TRAP

Cover to stop birds and rain from getting in

Staple here

Staple here

Sunk in level with ground

Converted top of bottle

Slippery sides

Bottom of bottle

BUTTERFLIES
WHY SHEER WONDER DOESN'T NEED A NAME

O n the page opposite are eight butterflies with which I hope you are largely familiar, if not by name then by sight, as these are all the species that are almost guaranteed as garden visitors. However, for me, butterflies are a perfect example of a group of animals that encourage both complacency and distracted obsession with nomenclature.

You see, whilst it is essential to be able to name something to effectively communicate, to become preoccupied with recognition and naming is a tragic waste of a naturalist's interest, an interest which is hopefully fuelled by the wonder of the thing he or she observes. Peacock or Comma, Brimstone or Orange Tip - so what? Consider those fragile planes of dusty tissue, veins so delicate - coloured so beautifully, those wings that flutter so crazily to keep these things airborne. Imagine those eyes - nearly half a head - each complex containing thousands of lenses. What do they see? How do they see? Do they see a thousand little different views or build all the images into one composite picture? And what about that mouth? No lips, no teeth, just a long coiled tongue - a watch spring with a nectar seeking tip - and the antennae, those two clubs, what do they sense? We can only imagine! And that's the key - get close to a butterfly, hold your breath, watch your shadow, creep in until your nose is ticklingly close and then look at it as you did all

Above, top left: Holly Blue female in repose, perhaps the daintiest darling. Left: Small Copper, glimmering glitz that's definitely not as common. Above: Painted Lady, a migrant from southern summers for whom Buddleia is a veritable magnet.

those years ago as a child. Don't ask its name, just ask questions you can't answer, and be in awe.

The butterfly bush

Buddleia is an easy to grow and prolific garden plant and is always a draw for many species of butterfly, including including all the Vannessids, the browns and the whites, not to mention a host of moths, flies, bees and wasps. Rotting fruit is also popular, especially in the autumn, so if you're orchardless try some Cox's apples, carved open and left in a sunny spot on the lawn. If no butterflies show up, at least my friends the wasps will have a feast!

Many species of animal and plant have different requirements throughout their lives, not just those that metamorphose such as butterflies. Nevertheless, careful consideration will need to be applied to cater for all stages, something that is often impossible on a garden-sized reserve. This is certainly the case for many butterflies particularly those woodland or grassland species that require maturity or miles of open space to prosper. Fortunately, the adult stages rarely refuse nectar so Buddleia will be a welcome refreshment centre.

COMMA

The ragged wings of the Comma are an effective camouflage when this insect is at rest. These butterflies are never as common as the Small Tortoiseshells and always strike me as a little more cautious when you are stalking them on their autumn favourites, Michaelmas Daisies.

SMALL TORTOISESHELL

Small Tortoiseshells overwinter here in the UK, typically hanging upside down in dry roofs, garages or sheds, emerging in March to claim the title of our most common brightly coloured butterfly. Their rich orange jerkins are nothing to be sneezed at, especially when a gang get going on a suitably nectarful clump.

PEACOCK

Peacock butterflies have two prominent 'eyes' on their forewings, similar to those that emblazon the tail feathers of the Peacock itself. This is another reason to pay only passing attention to the biological naming process. It is almost totally devoid of humour and imagination!

RED ADMIRAL

With its broad scarlet ribbons and thick velvety body, the Red Admiral is a favourite summer migrant to the UK, having escaped the fierce Mediterranean sun. Individual insects may frequent the same flowers at the same time each day before flying off to roost in a tree for the night.

WHITES

The Whites are blighted with 'pest' status and discourtesy, being overlooked as obvious, common and plain. But for myself the Cuckoo is a poor harbinger of spring, compared with the flaming, sulphurous wings of a male Brimstone (top) bouncing across suburbia, setting March ablaze with simple colour. Large and Small Whites (middle) have larvae that nourish themselves upon cabbages and their allies, but a little hole here and there is a small price to pay for a garden full of these aerial blossoms, fluttering prettily from the vegetable patch to the patio. Green-Veined Whites are more partial to Charlock and Rape, so they're someone else's problem. Orange Tips (bottom) are simply beautiful, a colour-by-numbers painting set from a six year old's fairytale.

SPECKLED WOOD

Speckled Woods are pretty dowdy but terribly exciting because they actually fight for the sunspots in glades and clearings. Males will repeatedly rise in the twinkling duels, jostling with each other until somehow one of them decides who has won. Whilst the victor settles in the sun, the loser languishes in the shade, out of heat and out of favour with any passing females.

MOTHS
NO CANDLES NEEDED TO SEE THE LIGHT

Crazed satellites crashing, burning up in arcs and buzzing and ending with a terminal thud and a dazed crawl into a dark corner. A myriad sparks whirring, as electrons around an atom, blinded and confused, tiny flies and midges with no names make up the firework crowd that the meteoric moths pass through as they gravitate into the trap. A Mercury Vapour lamp moth trap is the entomologist's master stroke. We place ours in an open area, switch it on at dusk, and its bright light immediately begins drawing moths, many from several kilometres away. They fly in, tumble into the funnel and hide in the bucket below, seeking shelter under the cups of cardboard egg cartons. By night it's the hottest disco in town, after sunrise the hangovers have set in and all is still. The anticipation is palpable. We wake before the alarm, drawn to the magic box to see what secrets it holds. The perspex cowl is lifted off and each egg tray examined; those 'special' species and a multitude of unknowns are coaxed with a paintbrush into plastic tubs ready for identification. The trophies are soon in a tray on the bottom of Mummy's bed and she is rudely awakened to find a Buff Tip or Poplar Hawk Moth centimetres from her moth-shocked nose.

These traps are ridiculously over-priced, the single most expensive piece of any naturalist's kit, but worth every penny. Buy, beg, steal or borrow one, and you'll see what I mean.

If not, build your own, using plastic tubs and bottles. Construct a funnel and holding chamber and place it under any garden light, the brighter the better. To increase its luminous appeal you can set the contraption on a white sheet to maximize the size of the beacon.

Generally, however, a more effective alternative to the MV trap is sugaring. This lure has been used since the Victorian age and recipes have three

Above: *Don't tell me that we've no exotics, Eyed Hawk Moth showing off its 'eyes' and looking totally tropical.*

essential ingredients; a sweetener, an aromatic attractant and some alcohol, intended to stupefy the moths. Try simmering real ale with brown sugar and molasses for about ten minutes. When the brew is cold add some rum or red wine and experiment with flavourings such as mashed bananas or apples. Pour the concoction into a bowl and leave a knotted towel or plaited cotton sheet to soak in it all day. Come the evening peg or tie it on to a tree, fence, wall or washing line at chest height and paint some of the remaining mixture onto any nearby tree trunks or fence posts. Check with a torch throughout the night. I tried sugaring several times as a child and not a single moth showed. Then a few years ago I joined a party of lepidopterists for a night in the New Forest, and clouds of insects appeared. I think my mum had been a bit mean with the rum!

Left: *Home made moth traps will focus the locals but fail to draw in animals from any great distance. I'm afraid that if you catch the 'mothing' bug you'll have to spend out.*

1 WHITE ERMINE MOTH

The White Ermine moth flies from late May until July with an occasional second generation in the autumn. This moth is a beautiful creamy white, variably spotted with dark chestnut and have the rear of their abdomen coloured yellow, something that is invisible when they are at rest. It can be found on walls, fences and trees but is normally noticed attending lights of all kinds. For me it's the 'Hamster' of the moth world, small, furry, quiet and sleepy.

2 HEART AND DART

Oh dear, the Heart and Dart. Hopeless and Dreary would be a better name if it weren't for the inconspicuous spots on the forewings of this moth which are allegedly heart and dart shaped. If a little brown moth that's been blown to bits crashes on your hall carpet to die anytime between the beginning of May and mid-August, it will almost certainly be one of these.

3 HERALD

The Herald is one of the last moths of the season. It flies from late July into November and again after hibernation when it 'heralds' spring, emerging in March and flying until June. Woodlands and gardens are its haunts and it is common everywhere except Scotland. Ivy blossom, ripe blackberries and light take its fancy, although you may find it hung up in sheds, barns, or the loft where it overwinters.

4 BRIMSTONE MOTH

In the south adult Brimstone moths are on the wing from April through to October, while in the north the principal flight time is during June and July. They can be found all over the UK, including most of the Scottish Islands. They fly at dusk and are always drawn to lights, often in great numbers.

5 CINNABAR MOTH

The Cinnabar Moth, a real dapper flapper, has vermilion hind wings and red spotted velvety grey forewings. Take care not to confuse this species with the day-flying Burnet moths, which are similarly hued.

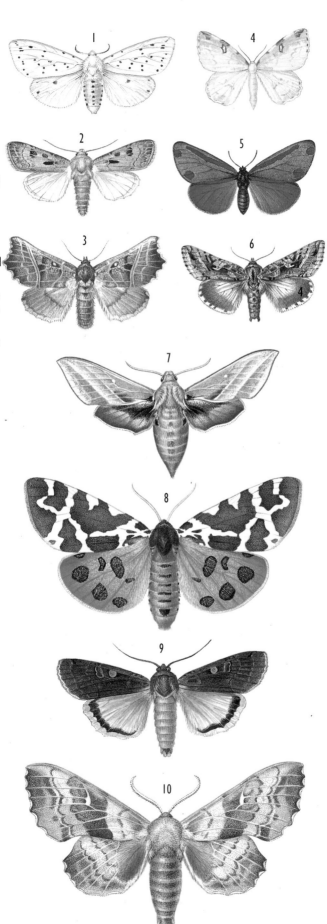

6 SILVER Y

Guess what the Silver Y has on its forewing? These are day flying summer visitors that arrive from late spring onwards and by late summer, when a British generation emerges, they can be extremely common. At rest the fragmented patterning and sculptured abdomen make this moth a triumph of concealment.

7 ELEPHANT HAWK MOTH

Both honeysuckle and rhododendron are said to attract Elephant Hawk moths when they are on the wing between May and July. Freshly emerged from the pupae and in prime condition they are contenders for the most beautiful of the British moths.

8 GARDEN TIGER MOTH

These bright, spotty and funky moths are very variable in colour and were once selectively bred by collectors to produce even more extreme variations. They are widespread and drawn to lights during July and August.

9 LARGE YELLOW UNDERWING

If anyone says, 'there's a whacking great moth going crazy in my kitchen/conservatory/toilet', tell them immediately that it's a Large Yellow Underwing. When they say, 'it hasn't got yellow under its wings', tell them it is actually difficult to see the rich ochre on the hind wings, because it's quite invisible at rest, and their wings beat too fast to see it in flight. Between July and September these moths are common and often vast numbers of migrants join us from the continent too.

10 POPLAR HAWK MOTH

Britain has nine residents and eight migrant Hawk moths on its list and in terms of size they are certainly our most exciting species. The Poplar Hawk moth is one of the most widely distributed and a moth which comes readily to light sources between May and July. At rest its pale brown, striped silvery grey wings act as perfect camouflage on any light bark or leaf debris. But if threatened it will jerk its fore-wings to reveal to dark crimson splashes on its underwings.

SPIDERS

Above: *Who'd choose to be a fly upon re-incarnation? Spiders are super predators. Some use sticky webs, some chase and pounce, others jump. Some even parachute around the countryside and many are extremely beautiful. Don't just spare them, spare them some time.*

I live with Arachnophobia nearly everyday of the year. Not me, of course, I've liked spiders all my life, but my girlfriend is rather severely afflicted. Now, in a spider-less environment this wouldn't present a problem, but very few such places exist. As a group the Arachnids have colonised virtually the entire globe, and our houses and gardens are no exception. At home we do little more to attract these creatures than leave our windows open, but this is invitation enough to a rich resource for foraging and breeding, and some species have made a niche for themselves behind the TV!

There are more than 80,000 species of spider worldwide, but fewer than 25 are known to be poisonous to humans and only a non-literal handful can be described as aggressive. None of the 350 larger species found in Britain fall into this category. I've been bitten by two of our resident spiders and said 'ouch'. Nothing more happened. All spiders are venomous. Being fragile, they use toxins rather than brawn to subdue their prey, but their venoms have evolved specifically to immobolise or kill that prey. Because none eat humans, few can do us any harm. They are a fabulously diverse group of animals of

which many are extremely beautiful and have fascinating life histories, so it is a pity that they are so widely vilified. Apparently it's their fast, scuttling movement, or their long, hairy legs, (which also accounts for the reasons many people don't like Manchester United I suppose!). Whatever you think of them, they are at – or near – the top of the invertebrate food chain, and thus, if you are not a fan of flies and most other things creeping and crawling, they will prove to be a valuable asset to your house or garden. There are many species of birds who are partial to spiders and a healthy population will prove a bonus to your Dunnocks, Robins, Thrushes and Wrens. So, all in all, it's worth encouraging spiders with patches of overgrown garden and a ban on insecticides. You can't have all of those pretty predators without their multi-legged prey.

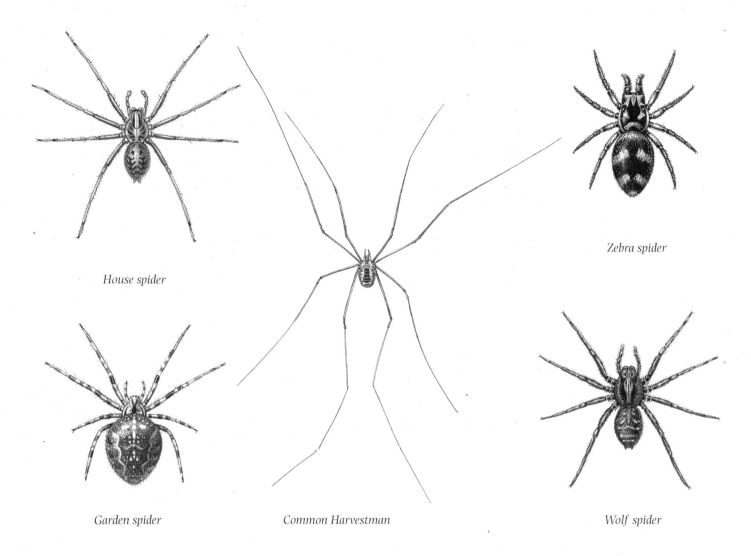

House spider

Zebra spider

Garden spider

Common Harvestman

Wolf spider

HOUSE SPIDER

I read some time ago that our common House Spider was the fastest spider in the world, able to sprint at up to four metres per second. It is a pursuit predator capable of making a meal from almost any invertebrate beneath your bookcase. The smaller males appear in early summer before giving way to the larger females, which mature in the autumn and can live for up to four years. Both are highly variable in colour, ranging from yellowish through to chocolate-brown. They are one of our largest spiders but like so many things their actual size is always exaggerated!

GARDEN SPIDER

Fat and fertile, hanging like a rich mouldy grape in the centre of her web feasting on the last of the season's fare, the female Garden Spider will prosper until the first hard frost cracks her plump body. September is her prime time, having long ago mated and deposited her batch of eggs ready to hatch in the spring. Patterned with bands and patches of ochres and reds, freckled with spots of chestnut and black and studded with diamonds of white she moults into a final coat of great finery, always reminding me of Henry VIII's brocaded waistcoats.

ZEBRA SPIDER

The black and white Zebra Spider can be commonly found on house walls, larger rockeries or occasionally on the trunks of mature trees. It is one of over four thousand jump-ing spiders and has exceptionally acute vision. Zebra Spiders stalk their prey to within a few centimetres and then leap onto it, readily capturing anything their own size. Males have an elaborate courtship dance which they perform for the female, but can be induced to dance with themselves if you place a mirror in front of them.

WOLF SPIDER

Wolf Spiders are, as their name suggests, large, robust predatory animals which roam over drier grassy areas at night. They don't howl! But they do excavate dens in which they secrete their white egg sacs and in which they remain until those eggs hatch. Males are smaller than females and both are active throughout the year.

COMMON HARVESTMAN

Leiobunum rotundum is probably our most common and widespread harvestman. It can be found in virtually any habitat between mid-summer and late autumn and, whilst males are smaller and reddish brown, the females are twice their size and generally lighter brown or beige with dark chestnut bars, spots and bands. Harvestmen are easily distinguished from most other spiders because their body parts are fused into one central oval node and they have absurdly long legs.

FLIES AND BEES

I am sure you have the general gist by now. I am a man who, in an almost Jainist manner, respects all animal life and quite literally wouldn't hurt a fly. I know this may be going too far for even the most dedicated naturalist, but then how many of us in some unoccupied moment have not focused on the antics of a group of houseflies gyrating like tiny scorched satellites about the room light. This electric sun and its cording becomes their focus of their activity as they speed senselessly on strict isometric courses, tracing triangles, squares and pentagons against the stark desert of the ceiling. At the apex of each line they imperceptably pause before an extraordinary acceleration whips them through another phase of their insane journey. Occasionally one hangs up its wings

Left: *A great pretender. This hoverfly is using the warning coloration of the wasp to fool potential predators into thinking it has a sting, when of course it hasn't. A common trick among such orders of insecta.*

on the lamp shade for a 'time out'. Another may join the party and be relentlessly attacked, the combatants combining magnetically and vanishing in a Kamekazi plummet to the rug miles below. A few seconds later, one resumes its course and so, hour after hour, this dainty display continues. More than once I have been relaxed by the tiny dancers and wished I was among them blasting my tiny airframe about that tatty old lampshade without a thought in my ephemeral little mind.

These darting cadets are males of the Lesser Housefly, and if spared for a few hours, or even indefinitely from chemical assault, their behaviour is free to enjoy from the comfort of your armchair. I appreciate that such charity maybe difficult because these animals are universally loathed. Their ability to spread diseases, including such treats as typhoid, cholera and dysentry has not made them many friends. Neither are their breeding habits very appealing to humans. Dung, sewage, preferably decaying, and rotting foods or flesh are the favourite environment in which houseflies abandon their eggs. On hatching, their larvae frolic in the ferment and grow rapidly so that in only a few days they are treading this stuff over your tables, food and forearms. Unsavoury maybe, but successful certainly, because, along with a few other 'pests, houseflies have spread the world over, amusing some and poisoning others. I can stop these animals from soiling my foodstuffs for a few pence, so in order to enjoy their madcap fly-pasts I'll spare them all summer long. For me they are far more entertaining than those busybodies that buzz amongst the Pegonias!

Above: *The Honeybee, probably everybody's favourite non-native with a sting. Strange how we forget fear for the price of some sweet stuff, but then it is a pollinator* par excellence *and so mild mannered that such violent eventualities are very rare.*

ROBBER FLY

Asilus crabroniformis is one of Britain's most impressive flies, a quite imposing, even fearsome creature, which is completely harmless to humans. Not so to insects, which it seizes in a short capture dart from its perch on twigs or stones. Grasshoppers, beetles, bees and wasps are all despatched and sucked dry. At rest its pose suggests that of a crouching cat, long legs folded for instant speed. Tiger Beetles and various hunting wasps get the better of them.

HOVERFLY

The *Volucella* genus of hoverflies are speedy and splendid, large, quite striking and obviously harmless. *V. zonaria* was once quite a prize for fly collectors, but recently has become common in the south and can be seen feeding on late summer blossoms, particularly bramble and ivy. However, it's actually the larvae which are most impressive — they inhabit the interiors of wasps', and bees' nests. Here they roam about unmolested until they squeeze inside a cell with a developing grub and excite it to secrete its excremental juices which they promptly eat! Now that's what I call wildlife!

HOUSE FLY

There are more than 450 species of this family of flies The true Housefly *Musca domestica* has a yellowy buff abdomen and various peculiar details in the veins of the wings. Females lay about nine hundred eggs and these can hatch in just eight hours and the larvae can mature and pupate in just under forty-eight. The main brood emerges in June or July and continues until September. As you depress the aerosol button, remember that if there wasn't a job for flies to do they wouldn't be there.

Robber fly

Hoverfly

House fly

Honey bee

Bumble bee

HONEY BEE

There is not a better known insect on Earth, with a library of books available on this species' behaviour, ecology, physiology and management. The three castes, queen, drone and worker, are easily distinguished, although it is only the worker that is typically encountered. A good colony can have more than fifty thousand bees, all of them workers, and these rarely live more than a few weeks in a busy summer season. During the winter the drones are ejected because they don't do anything and the colony settles down to rest, feeding on the stored pollen and honey. Isn't it amazing how we all love 'busy bee' because it gives us honey, yet the poor old wasp is a pest?

BUMBLE BEE

The bumble or humble bees are also social, building their far smaller nest under ground. Only the queens survive the winter to start a new colony by making a small tablet of 'bee bread' from pollen and nectar onto which they lay ten to twelve eggs. All hatch to become workers and they take over the task of feeding the forthcoming grubs for which the queen builds the cells. At the end of the summer males and females emerge, mate, and then the males die. There are fewer than thirty British species, typically named after the colour of their tails. Imaginative, eh?

PONDS

HISTORY OF PONDS

It strikes me as sad that today most of us regard ponds as 'ornamental garden features'. We forget how important a role they have played in our social history and how at one time they were an essential centrepiece for each human community, not just a refuge for invertebrates. Defined as a small body of still water, ponds are normally man-made features. Water is essential to any human settlement and natural hollows were probably 'improved' by being lined with puddled clay and topped with flint to prevent animals hooves puncturing this sealant.

Farmers dug 'farm' and 'field' ponds to water the grazing stock and drain their land; many a monastery or mansion had its 'stew pond' where fish, typically carp, were farmed to provide an alternative to meat on fast days. Ponds formed where any excavation was made; clay, gravel and peat pits all filled with water and may have acted as flighting ponds attracting wildfowl which were caught in elaborate decoy nets. Roadside ponds refreshed travellers and their horses and served to swell their cartwheels which otherwise shrank and shed their iron tyres. Those guys aboard Constable's Haywain hadn't lost control on a tricky bend and skidded in to that famous Essex waterhole – they'd parked it there deliberately!

Mill ponds, designed to hold a good head of water above the mill stream to power water wheels, which in turn turned the stones over the corn, were also common. But all this is history, and first to go from the village was its pond. As soon as piped water stretched into the countryside, the marginal vegetation grew unchecked and a circle of rushes was all that remained, even that now buried beneath a wider road or a new estate which covers the old green. The field ponds were filled to make mechanical farming easier and wayside water is not a motorway necessity. And now, like the ponds, we've neglected the village store, the post office and the pub, and all paid the price socially. Without

focal points how can any human community function in a friendly way?

Some rural areas seem to have fared better. I once climbed to a castle perched high over Cheshire in pursuit of Peregrine Falcons and as the sun set I watched hundreds of pools glow gold in the surrounding fields. In the last few years the problems facing our desiccating countryside have been brought to the fore and conservationists regularly liaise with the newly privatized water companies to reduce abstraction from rivers, waterways and subterranean water tables. There are too few reservoirs, and our most essential resource just drains away. We lobby for reason, but everyone is thirsty and wasteful, and unfortunately our ponds and streams are vanishing. So, as usual, it's down to us as individuals to take control. Garden ponds rarely need planning permission, so if you want one you can have one. If you have the will you can make a little corner of Britain wetter. And keep it wet – no infilling, no abstraction – and it will make a difference because so many species of plant and animal need only a small body of water to thrive or survive. Some are already dependent on garden ponds, so sharpen the spade – your species need you!

A BUCKET FOR LIFE

Here is an enchanting idea – buy a plastic bucket and start life on Earth. Ingredients required: only water. As we all know, the rainy wet stuff is essential to all life, and life therefore seeks it out, even in the most harsh environment. A yellow plastic bucket filled with treated tap water may not seem a particularly hospitable habitat but if you place one on your windowsill or doorstep and check it once a day you'll see it transform into a remarkable little microcosm. Okay, initially it will be very slow and you'll need a microscope to see the pioneers – simple animals such as *amoebae* and *ciliates*, single-celled organisms which can arrive in raindrops or be blown in dust or on fragments of leaves too tiny to see. Their meagre nutrients will fatten an army of equally minute predators that follow them in. Flies, bees and wasps, craneflies or perhaps slugs and woodlice will amble by in search of a sip and, with characteristic carelessness, will topple in, drown and quickly decay, freeing their mixture of bodily molecules to enrich the primal soup. Algal spores will blow in and prosper and as the sides of your bucket darken with green slime, legions of little herbivores will arrive to graze on this new salad.

I admit that *Monads*, *Choanoflagellates*, *Rhizopodes*, *Heliozodes* and *Loxodes*, collectively protozoans, are not big news in the wildlife terms. But bigger things soon follow, notably worms (wow!). Flat worms, ribbon worms, round worms, horse hair worms and segmented worms will all wriggle in the sediment as *Tardigrades* and crustaceans paddle in the middle depths. Then what about mosquito larvae? The floating boats of eggs hatch into rapidly growing cylindrical larvae.

Above and left:
Metamorphosis is always close to miraculous even when it involves mosquitoes. In just a few days these tube-breathing larvae will emerge as winged adults and not every species will be flying straight for your jugular.

Left: *Water louse. Not as exciting as a Tiger but commoner and equally valuable in the web of life. Without them we'd have ponds full of dead leaves.*

These spend most of their time hanging on the surface with their breather tube while filter feeding with their brush-like mouthparts. A tap to the rim produces an immediate antipredator response – they dive with a violent wriggling action. The mobile, comma-shaped pupae do the same. Watching these humble creatures in an old baby bath was my introduction, aged three or four, to the incredible phenomenon of metamorphosis. To this day I can't resist aggravating a larva and recently sat with another fascinated four-year old and watched a pupa peel apart and the adult mosquito emerge. We were enraptured by a little thing appearing from merely water to play its role in the great scheme of things. To witness it for the price for a plastic bucket should, in my opinion, be mandatory for all because when you come down to it, all you need for a miracle on your street is a mosquito!

Microscopes

Microscopes are not out of the question. My father bought one for four pounds at a car boot sale recently. It was crude, a mirror-operated affair fabricated somewhere in the Russian federation. But it worked; we looked through

it and all saw things that we couldn't see with our naked eyes and whether you're five or forty-five that's what's important. We watched *Daphnia* the size of cars, forests of algae, some *Hydra* and some fat ciliates buzzing around with their pretty rainbows of swimming hairs and by teatime we'd all had more then four pounds' worth. Shop secondhand and see a little world bigger!

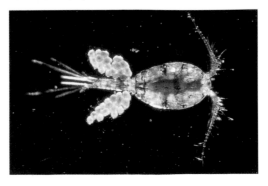

Above: '*My newt's bigger than yours.*' '*I caught the diving beetle.*' '*Your tad-pole has only one eye.*' '*It's not a drag-onfly nymph, it's a dinosaur larva.*' *Familiar pond-side banter recalled.*

Left: *This tiny symmetrical organism is* Cyclops *and is common in almost all waters. All you need to explore the extraordinary mini-fauna of a puddle is a cheap microscope – don't miss out.*

93

POND DESIGN

Above: *What a beauty! I wish this pond were mine. It looks superb – a perfect example of what can so easily be achieved with a little hard work.*

Watching life colonize a bucket is a neat experiment but I am sure you will want to do more and one of the most fundamental ways to improve your patch as a wildlife resource is to put a pond in it. An old bath sunk into the lawn will be used by all sorts of animals, but its steep sides and small size will preclude others and inhibit its value. For instance, frogs may well choose to spawn in it when it's deep and brimming with water in March, but the emerging froglets will have real trouble scaling its sides in the summer. When it comes to ponds the rule is that big is better. As a guide, most big exciting dragonfly species require a pond of at least 40 sq m while some of the smaller ones can cope with 4 sq m.

A few factors you should consider include the presence of trees, firstly because ponds need a sunny aspect, and secondly because of the build up of leaf litter in the pond. Unless this is regularly removed, something which invariably disturbs the whole ecology, it leads to enrichment and stagnation. Shelter from prevailing winds is desirable, perhaps a wall or fence can achieve this, or you could make a bank from the soil you remove in the process of digging. Siting the edge of your pond on the very boundary of your property is counter-productive. It makes access difficult for cleaning and exploring, and it limits the amount of pondside vegetation that might be available, a necessary resource for many creatures.

It is worth reducing the size of your pond to accommodate a marshy area, a lagoon filled with rushes and sedges saves more space for an open water section and diversifies the habitat. Always think about accessibility too, if you dig the pond right outside the backdoor you'll need a bridge to get over to the lawn, and remember that you'll need to get to the edge for a bit of pond dipping, so maybe this should be adjacent to an existing path or patio. Also bear in the mind that not all the creatures that will colonize your oasis will want to be seen every time you play cricket or have a Barbeque. Offering an area which allows them some distance and privacy from your comings and goings will be welcome.

A good idea is to get a long length of brightly coloured nylon rope or ribbon, or a garden hose-pipe and lay it on the ground to mark the outline of your proposed pond. Then get a beer and mull it over. Show the rest of the household and see if they have any good ideas. Try different shapes and see how you can complement the design with existing features in the garden. Think three dimensionally; steep sides or sharp corners should be avoided, if you are going to use a mechanical digger consider its access, and perhaps most important of all, to avoid major embarrassment, find out if there are any water, gas or telephone lines running beneath your chosen spot.

Next, think about depth. Remember that some shallow areas are vital. If the whole pond is shallow, less than 20 cm, it will heat up in summer, reducing the oxygen content, or even dry up altogether and in winter it could freeze to the bottom and kill everything you are trying to encourage. A gently sloping shelf, at least 20 or 30 cm out into the pond is mandatory, as many species will enjoy the warmer water. A minimum depth of 60 cm is desirable over some extensive area of the pond as a deep water refuge and 75 cm or more is better for ponds over 20 sq m. Lastly, draw some simple diagrams and attempt to calculate the actual area of the pond, as this will relate to the expense of construction. Modify your plans accordingly by expanding or contracting your hose-pipe outline.

POND CONSTRUCTION

There are five basic types of pond, three of which are likely to be inappropriate. If you have a permanently high water table, or your garden is on impervious clay you may only need to dig a hole which will fill with water. If you have access to a huge amount of fine clay you could construct a puddled clay pond. This would be cheap but involve a huge amount of hard and messy work -- something for the medieval traditionalist! There are pre-formed liners, which make fine ornamental ponds or small fishponds, but their steep sides make them unsuitable as a wildlife pond.

This leaves us with concrete or plastic- or rubber-lined ponds. Concrete ponds are difficult and expensive to install. A wire cage is needed, as is an expert at using the material, which needs to be skilfully and speedily applied in good weather. Then it needs chemical waterproofing and draining and re-filling several times to prevent any toxic residue contaminating the water. Damage due to freezing is frequent around the edges and if a more serious leak appears it can be tricky to mend. So, the best, easiest and cheapest approach is a plastic or rubber lining, and the key to success like so much DIY, is in the preparation.

Polythene is cheap and easy to fit but even a three-ply fabric will not last very long. Personally, I'd spend out on butyl rubber (isobutylene isoprene). It's normally guaranteed for at least twenty years, is at least 1.75 mm thick and is thus more resistant to puncturing. If your pond plans are lake-ish, you may wish to compromise with rubberised plastic (ethylene propylene diene), which is cheaper and a little less flexible. Water garden centres sell these materials off the roll or in sheets and for small ponds I'd

Left & below: How to make a mud pit. Don't be disappointed when you finish, nature takes time and a couple of years are needed for the pond to settle in. If you have as many friends as this guy, you'll be lucky.

shop around for the best deal. But if you are thinking big (20 metres square plus) I'd go direct to the manufacturer.

Now the hard part. Dig your hole, either mechanically (nice) or like a navvy (not very nice). I know it's not my place to say it, but watch your back. Next, rake the surface and remove all stones, twigs and roots. Don't economize here, get down on muddy hands and knees and pick over the entire surface. Coat the entire area to be covered with the liner with at least 6 cm depth of fine sifted sand and this in turn with wetted newspapers, carpet felt, or underlay or old carpet itself.

Now measure up. A fair guide for the length of liner required is equal to the actual length, plus twice the maximum depth, plus 50 cm. Width equals actual width plus twice maximum depth, plus 50 cm. Remember to add more if you plan for marshy lagoons.

The lining is then laid, not stretched, over the hole and gently moulded to fit by pleating in creases. If it goes wrong lift it out and start again, repairing any damage. When you are satisfied, secure the sides either by topping off with stone slabs or by digging a trench about 30–40 cm from the intended edge and burying the outside edge of the liner, to be later covered with turf. Only at the very end cut away any wastage.

Fill the pond at a trickle to allow the weight of water to stretch and adapt the lining to the bottom and leave it standing for two or three days to allow for chlorine levels to diminish before plants or animals are introduced.

PLANTING YOUR POND

Left and below: *Lilies, white and yellow, are a favourite with both the aesthete and the invertebrate. Do not allow them to swamp the entire pond. Grub out annually.*

Standing in the mud, looking at the crater you've spent ages designing and digging, nothing could be more disappointing. Its bland, primal nakedness, its wretched trampled rim, the scummy soupy water are so different from your daydreams of a verdant, clear pool buzzing with life. But then any fool can dig a hole, the skill is in crafting it into a reality, and that means a good planting plan.

The vegetation of ponds can be divided into a series of zones, each suitable for distinctly different species. The skill is to meld a mix of species from each of these zones that will provide for the greatest diversity of other, i.e. animal, life. In a natural system the first colonizers would be submerged waterweed. Next floating weeds appear and shade out those below and thus begins a gradual process of silting. Simultaneously, emergent swampy species will get a grip, and slowly constrict the perimeter of the pond. Marsh plants at its rim will exacerbate this and eventually a swamp will exist where once there was open water. Bushes and trees follow *en route* to dry land. This phenomenon is called succession, and to keep a pond a pond you'll need to dredge and dig out the encroaching swamp. However, that's a few years away from your bombsite. Let's first consider which green bits should grow where.

Canadian Pond Weed can be purchased from any water garden centre and despite being an alien species is a good starter. When it first appeared in 1840 it grew rampantly, clogging waterways country-wide, and when you plant a few stems in your pond it will invariably do the same. However, it will soon die back to manageable levels and is worth having because of its oxygenating qualities. Root it in spring; it will overwinter as shoots and begin flowering the next summer. Despite these blooms, it always develops vegetatively.

Water Milfoil, either spiked or whorled, is a similar species that enjoys more alkaline waters. They too will proliferate if conditions suit and overwinter with specialized buds or rhizomes. The smaller starworts, of which there are a few species, are another group to add to this bouquet. A mix of species is the best option so try to gather a little material, a plastic cup full each time you visit a neighbour's pond. For these sorts of species harbour no

guilt – they are capable of rapid growth and will not notice your pruning.

Next are plants rooted in the bottom mud but with floating leaves, the most obvious of which are the water lilies. There are two common species, the white and the yellow, and both produce dense rhizome root mats in the mud. If you're up to it (and it can be a grimy struggle) then cut out a few short sections of this, preferably with a few buds in spring time and pin them down in your pond bottom. String tied to a stone will do the trick. In summer long flexible stems will sprout the waxy water repellent leaves and the characteristic and attractive flowers. Seedpods are the result and these too can be harvested to help colonize your pool. Fringed Water Lily is a similar species, with neat round leaves. Water Crowfoot can provide a beautiful veil of white flowers to cover the surface in May and June, Arrowhead with its distinctive leaves and spikes of purple and white florets and the Broad-leaved Pond Weed which can smother the surface, are all suitable species to try. Some will run riot – don't be afraid to cut them back as your aim is to create a habitat mosaic with as many different species as possible. All are suitable species to hold egg masses or larvae or colonies of smaller animals, some of which may be species specific – without the plant, you won't get the animal.

Next are the floating plants with unanchored roots. Water Soldier is rare in natural ponds and should therefore be sourced from garden centres, where it is always available. Frogbit is a mat-forming species with leaves like a miniature water lily, which needs tight control along with the duck weeds, which are likely to arrive of their own accord. The latter group with their tiny bi-lobed leaves often form a rich green layer across the entire surface. This is an indication that the water is too rich in nutrients, or polluted, and such growth is as undesirable as that of the algae, *Spirogyra* and *Cladophora*.

The fringing vegetation of your pond is important on several accounts: it is more visible to you, essential for those species that need to climb in and out of the water and for all those semi-aquatic species that need the water only occasionally, such as the amphibians that return there to breed. The swampy species which tolerate partial immersion include bulrush, reedmace and the common reed. These look great, indeed few self-respecting ponds sit proud without a clump of these poker-headed plants at their side, but they produce such an abundance of leaf litter that consolidates among their dense rhizomes each winter, that unchecked they will soon suck your pond dry. Aggressive grubbing is needed each year, and if you slack for a season then cutting out the resultant mat becomes hard and muddy work. Take heed! Branched Burweed, Water Plantain, Water Mint, Bogbean, Marestail and Watercress all occur in the marshy fringe, along with sedges, irises and marigolds. Many of these plants have showy flowers, the Kingcup for example, and as such they're a must for the fauvists.

There are two prime considerations when planting a pond. Firstly, there is no need to overspend or overcollect when you start. It is easier and more satisfying to add material than it is to take it out. Secondly, don't expect to get it right straight away. Your pond will need time to settle down, you may get a bloom of Duck Weed, the Canadian Pond Weed may appear to threaten your life and your water lilies may all die. The nutrients of the system will need to equilibrate and the first few species to get a hold will have a stabilizing influence. Unfortunately, you may have to sit back for that first summer and endure trophic anarchy and it could be two or three more years before your pond begins to match the fantasy in your mind's eye. Nevertheless, when your first spawn ball appears or when a brilliant blue damselfly first zips over the fence and onto your oasis, it will all be worth the wait.

Left: *All you want and more – an idealistic vision of pond life that you could turn into reality.*

Sympetrum Dragonfly
Iris
Gnat
Pond Skater
Whirligig Beetles
Spiked Water Milfoil
Froglet
Hornwort
Common Frog
Water Stick Insect
Water Scorpion
Lesser Water Boatman
Canadian Pondweed
Worm Leech
Water fleas
Great Ramshorn Snail
Caddis Fly larva
Common Newt
Great Pond Snail
Great Diving Beetle
Dragonfly nymph

PLANTS

GREEN BITS

In terms of ecological fundamentals this should be page one. Plants of all kinds are classed as primary producers. They use the sun's energy, and water, to assimilate carbon dioxide from the air and convert it into sugars, thus releasing them from a need for an external source of carbohydrate. Animal life cannot do this and therefore nothing can exist without plants somewhere in its food chain. So why are the 'green bits' buried in the middle of this book? Simply because most of us perceive birds, mammals, insects and all the rest to be more interesting than the likes of grass, moss or algae. Despite the wonders of their blooms, the inventiveness of their seed dispersal mechanisms or the diversity which permits plants to grow almost anywhere on Earth, plants seem destined to be firmly rooted at the foot of any naturalist's interests.

Not long ago, I had the good fortune to visit Cuba and enjoy two great botanical moments. Firstly, I stood in a hot and humid orchidarium and witnessed one of the most remarkable examples of biology I've ever seen.

A rather dull but elaborately constructed orchid flower had a tiny see-saw plinth at the mouth of its nectary. It was not only a guard but also a selecting mechanism. Flies fancy a sip of nectar and are attracted by a specific scent, but if they are too big or too heavy, the fulcrum flips quickly and they fail to get in. If they are too small or too light, it won't flip at all and the nectary remains closed. Only one species of fly has the exact right size and weight ratio to see-saw into the nectary where it effects the pollination of the orchid as a by-product of its hunger. We stood and watched a little red-eyed green jewel do just this. In a great big rich and distant jungle we saw one fly interact essentially with one plant and all took our sweaty hats off to evolution. It made me feel small, inconsequential and the perfection of it was almost embarrassing.

If that was good biology, I also encountered great romance. I visited a garden full of exotic trees which had been initially planted over a hundred years ago. The daughter of its founder still lives there in a charismatic and cluttered cottage, the walls of which were papered with magazine photographs. I peeped around and saw

Above and left: *The awesome Military Orchid* (left) *is a national rarity that sprouts at secret locations and is strictly wardened. The striking dandelion* (above) *probably grows on your lawn (given the chance). Never allow familiarity to breed contempt. Beauty is in the eye of the bed-wetter.*

Sophia Loren and a young Kirk Douglas yellowing above her bed. The old, indeed ancient, lady courteously showed us around and patiently forgave my pidgin Spanish as I asked her about each of the beautifully tended plants and trees. At last she stopped by a real giant, stretched out a wizened hand to its less crinkled bark and gazed up into the mistiness of its high canopy. It was a beauty and I asked her how old she thought it was. 'Eighty-two,' she replied instantly. She had planted it with her father, aged eight, in 1917. How many of us could plant a tree with our children and know they'd still be loving and caring for it eighty years later, indeed how many of you older readers can boast this today? Surely few. Our world moves too fast for trees today, the measures we make in our gardening plans are more dot.com than decades and as a consequence we forsake the chances of our roles in such fairytales.

WANTED-WEEDS!

Shrivelling and pathetic she was, wobbling between the 'Flowerpot Men', whittering on in a puerile voice about nothing of consequence. 'Little Weed' was the least enigmatic of the trio.

Botanically, 'weed' doesn't mean weak, fragile, insignificant or ineffectual at all; it refers to anything 'that grows profusely amongst cultivated plants, depriving them of space or food etc'. It is a survivor and it's a telling paradox that we have had to spend countless millions developing and using horrible herbicides to obliterate the perfection of nature. The downside is that in our insane desire to do so we have ruined the countryside.

'Weeds' use various strategies to succeed. They produce vast quantities of tiny and mobile seeds which can lie dormant for many years (poppies). They germinate first or produce rapidly growing shoots that outperform other species and stretch up into the light before shading out their competitors (nettles). They are tolerant of extremely poor soils and prosper where others struggle (groundsels and ragworts) or they spread vegetatively using the strength of the 'parent' plant to swamp any other struggling seedlings (bracken, thistles). Non-natives can run riot in an ecosystem where the conditions for their growth are identical to their own but where no regulators such as herbivores or diseases have evolved (valerian and aubrietia). Some are resistant to trampling (plantains, silverweeds), others resistant to grazing because their essential growing points are so low or protected in the very base of the plant (the grasses). Whatever the secret of their success, 'weeds' are useful because of their sheer volume – they produce a huge amount of edible material very quickly and fill the stomachs of an army of herbivores. Nectar, seeds, shoots, leaves or roots are all gleaned by an extensive diversity of species.

Above: *Purple then prickly, Teasels are an attractive species which feed insects and then finches. When you've had enough, give them to granny for one of her dust-collecting, fire-hazard flower arrangements.*

Left: *Tolerance doesn't necessarily mean lack of control. Some species, here Golden Rod, will run amok if left unchecked. Every couple of years re-appraise the situation and make the cuts.*

Consider the thistle; a spiky and ferocious competitor to us but a salad for snails, a 'pub' for insects and a seed centre for finches. Tolerate a few in your garden and you'll make a lot of little things happy. And that's what it's all about, tolerance. You won't be farming in your garden; you don't need a crop. Why not a spattering of daisies and plantains on your lawn? Both are tolerant of mowing – that's why they're there. If you want to smash nature completely you could lay an 'Astro-turf' lawn? You won't need to weed, water or mow and it will be uniform for ever, perfect for the eco-fascist, a 'final solution' for all of your gardening worries.

Meanwhile, why not go organic and reject the use of chemicals in the garden? You can put weeds in their place by planting species which outcompete them to such an extent that manual control, 'pulling', will suffice. I have met a few keen gardeners who haven't used chemicals for years and their gardens look superb. But then if you enjoy wildlife these are unnecessary directions; you will want weeds because you will want what naturally comes with them. We rave about glades of foxgloves, groves of bluebells, beds of primroses, even verges of ox-eye daisies and we can with a little effort and planning have versions of all of these and more on our own patches. Think about it – I bet it will grow on you!

WEEDS YOU WANT

RED VALERIAN

This Mediterranean refugee has long escaped from our gardens and naturalized itself in Britain as far north as mid-Scotland. It likes dry, even stony soils and produces a great show of flowers between June and August. It is the perennial that anyone can grow, a fantastic nectar source for butterflies and moths and will add an immediate splash of colour to any garden.

MICHAELMAS DAISY

A native of the Eastern US seaboard that was introduced to Britain around 1710, it occurs in more than seventy different cultivars and is a perennial that flowers from August right through to early November. Thus it provides a superb late summer nectar source for wayside and garden butterflies. Like Valerian it prefers poor, well drained soils and is easy to establish and maintain. No garden should be without it.

FIELD SCABIOUS

Pollinated by bees and butterflies, this perennial favours chalky soils and would be an arable 'weed' were it not poisoned out of existence almost everywhere it tries to grow. It hangs on to road verges, hedge banks and areas of rough grassland. It flowers from July to September and is another favourite of butterflies, particularly the whites and browns.

FRAGRANT EVENING PRIMROSE

Another invader, this species has colonized roadsides, verges, waste grounds, sand dunes, and railway embankments as far north as Yorkshire. A biennial, it flowers from June to September and adds a flamboyant splash of yellow while supplying nectar to night-flying moths.

Red Valerian *Michaelmas Daisy*

Field Scabious

Common Knapweed

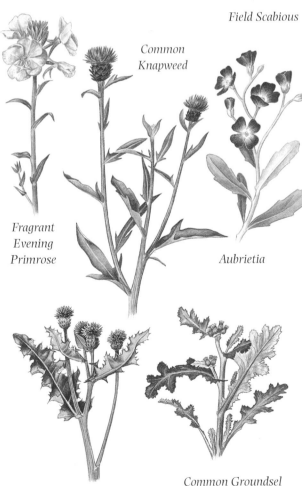

Fragrant Evening Primrose

Aubrietia

Creeping Thistle

Common Groundsel

COMMON KNAPWEED

Otherwise known as 'hard heads', this species occurs all over the UK on heavier and wetter soils. It favours meadows, rough grasslands, pastures and roadsides where it flowers from June to September and attracts a wide variety of larger insects — hoverflies, bumble bees and butterflies being the most obvious. It is a member of the thistle family but as it is not too aggressively armed it makes a good addition to the garden's edge.

AUBRIETIA

A native of the Eastern Mediterranean where it is an alpine species favouring rocks and scree, this species is commoner in gardens than out, although it has escaped onto a few dry wasteground sites. It's a perennial that flowers early in April and May and thus is a great early nectar source for overwintering adult butterflies and is very easily established in any open sunny location.

CREEPING THISTLE

This plant is common all over the UK and was included in the Weeds Act of 1959. It spreads by means of creeping lateral roots and requires thousands of tons of herbicides a year to control its spread onto any fertile arable fields. It thrives on meadows, roadsides and waste grounds where it flowers between July and September and attracts a magnificent array of insects. Best in a large garden where frequent strimming, not chemicals, can control its vegetative energies.

COMMON GROUNDSEL

This 'weed' likes heavier soils, where it is common and highly successful. It is an annual that flowers throughout the year and its small tufty flowers attract a range of smaller, perhaps less interesting, insects. Indeed the plant itself is not much of a looker so it's best included in an arable 'weed' scrape rather than actively encouraged all over the garden.

WILDFLOWERS
MEADOWS OR METRES SQUARED

Over the years I might have seen more wildflower 'meadows' than most. Squeezed into school grounds, the side of carparks, and the corners of tiny gardens, most were more metres than meadows but all worthy of merit. Sadly, quite a few people fail to realize that meadows don't remain meadows without mowing or grazing or ploughing, without annual management. Nevertheless, if you fancy recreating a little patch of an increasingly ancient landscape pick up your rake and turn your hand to your land.

As with most things, planning and preparation are essential. I spoke to the Landlife charity whose prosperous corporate partner Landlife Wildflowers is one of the few reputable merchants of seeds and flowers in the UK. Gill Watson, one of fourteen full-time staff, told me that strictly native stock are sourced and cultivated on their thirty-five hectare site near The National Wild Flower Centre at Knowsley near Liverpool. Landlife share research with Plantlife and work with other urban charities such as The Ground Work Trust, but also offer fabulous packages for the wildlife gardener with their carefully selected seed mixes. Gill says that many people initially have the wrong ideas about meadows; they imagine it's all about cornflowers, corncockles and poppies, basically all the glamour, when of course it's as much about grasses and less flamboyant flowers.

In a garden context I'm sure that most people will be keen on a bit of colour and there are plenty of mixes available to fill a small palette. It is unlikely that your 'field' will be fallow so the first task is to dig out all the existing vegetation. The majority of urban soils will be too fertile. You will need to remove nutrients and clear the site, so try covering the area with black polythene for a season, perhaps lifting it a couple of times to allow the natural seed bank to germinate and then replacing it to kill the seedlings. If this is not enough to sterilize and de-fertilize your soil you can remove it, or at least remove the fertile top layer, or use herbicide. Glyphosate-based chemicals are approved by English Nature as 'eco-friendly' herbicides; 'Tumbleweed' and 'Roundup' will kill off the less tenacious weeds, 'Broadshot' will hit thistle and docks harder and 'Klout' or 'Fusillade' will remove unwanted grasses.

It is essential that the soil is worked into a fine, dry crumb structure prior to sowing and that it is rolled after-

Above: *Monet would have loved this. Ox-eye daisies dominate a small meadow, and make me wonder who dreamt up the ridiculous idea of lawns in the first place. Answers on a postcard please.*

wards to ensure a good soil-seed contact. Sowing rates vary between species and mixes but one thing is for sure, although this is not a financially expensive undertaking, to work properly it requires good preparation and careful and continual management. Not all mixes will instantly burst into colour, some will require two or three years, some longer; for instance bluebells may need six years to produce a flowering bulb. If you are sowing by hand, mix the seeds with sand or sawdust so you can see where you have scattered.

Once plants are established, cutting regimes and timings are critical; many mixes/swards require only one cut late in the summer. As a non-gardener, I must with honesty refer you to other texts at this point:. *Wildflowers Work – A Technical Guide To Creating And Managing Wildflower Landscapes* by Lickorish, Luscombe and Scott is published by Landlife and appears to be just the job for larger scale projects. If your meadow is more of a patch than a field *How To Make Wild Flower Habitat Gardens*, is an excellent guide in Landlife's commercial catalogue. Seed mixes and advice are available for a range of soil types and shade conditions and the potential results look spectacular. Even I may be tempted to pick up a spade!

BUSHES TO BEAT ABOUT

What your garden really needs is spatial heterogeneity. It is one of the key ingredients to a rich biodiversity; rainforests have huge amounts of it and it isn't difficult to come by, but what is it?

You walk on a heath, across a meadow or through a wood – the difference is profound. Spatial heterogeneity translates to the filling of space using different physical means. A meadow may be rich in species but few grow above waist height, which is a waste of sky. Because nature doesn't suffer 'waste' easily we have bushes and then trees, growth forms that have evolved to exploit the lowest part of the sky. So to get some spatial heterogeneity you need bushes and trees.

My favourite bush is the **elder**. It is found throughout the British Isles. It is a pioneering shrub and will colonize any broken sandy ground, often occurring on dunes and around rabbit warrens. It also prospers on fertile calcareous soils, particularly if there has been some nitrogen enrichment. Thus old rubbish dumps, bonfire sites and riversides are frequently covered in dense elder growth. It is a deciduous species which produces dense umbels of flowers in June and July, these have been used for wine and champagne but are better exploited by a huge diversity of insects, notably flies, hoverflies and beetles. Remember, even if you're not a fly fancier, many birds are.

Elder can grow to 10 m in height but is best kept lower and bushier, say around 4-5 m maximum. This ensures that its rich foliage provides better cover for a huge range of nesting birds which may include Blackbirds, Song Thrushes, Robins, Wrens, Greenfinches, Chaffinches, Bullfinches and Goldfinches, plus a range of warblers and doves. It also readily 'hollows', so I've also found hole nesters such as the tits and even Tree Sparrows ensconced within its rotting trunks. In August and September its berries ripen to black and the bush becomes a bonanza. Thrushes predominate, but birds such as Blackcaps can be found picking through the clusters and come nightfall no Wood Mouse or Bank Vole in the area forsakes this feast.

A close second in the Best Bush Awards is the **hawthorn**, only its slower growth rate preventing a dead heat. Also known as 'May tree', or 'white- or quickthorn' it is similarly widespread and produces an abundance of blooms in May and berries, and haws in September. Both are a great draw for pretty much the same spread of species but the hawthorn's foliage is eaten by a few more larvae, including those of many moths.

Holly planted near to the house may ward off lightning but it is also slow-growing and not so productive on the berry front. **Cotoneaster** is in fact a native berry-bearer, but exotic varieties are more popular and, along with firethorn, are richly fruiting and provide good nesting cover at the expense of being vegetatively inert – nothing eats them.

Although not a bush by any means, **honeysuckle** can be a fantastic bonus. It tolerates all kinds of soils but likes them well drained and produces attractive 'hands' of richly scented flowers as it climbs. These are pollinated by night-flying moths, including the hawkmoths and by bumblebees. Prune it hard to produce dense nesting cover.

Left: Fully loaded Hawthorn; the thrushes can't wait.

Below left: Honeysuckle blossom and berries. Bees, butterflies, caterpillars and birds will all benefit, and Dormice even strip the bark to make their nests. Of course the scent is subtle, but divine.

Above: Elder – winner of the best bush award, here drooping 'umbels' of tasty berries. Try to leave some for the wildlife.

BUDDLEIA AND NETTLE SPECIAL

There is something so 'Disney' about a buddleia bush in July. The vulgar colour, bulbous blooms, sickly smell, and reeling chaos of crassly coloured butterflies, really smacks of a come-to-life-candy-castle in a cartoon. It's all so gaudy, so childish, so summery and definitely rude. I bet if Red Admirals could talk they'd be goin' "Aw right mate, look at the wings on that tortoiseshell", the tortoiseshell meanwhile dancing around the mauve cone -- like a disco dolly around a white patent leather handbag. "Oh yeah, that admiral bloke's a bit of alright, ain't he?". Every now and then a gang of drunk lads comes wasping around going " 'ere we buzz, 'ere we buzz, 'ere we buzz". By half past eleven in the morning they are all nectared out of their brains and trying to sleep off the debauched riot in the shade of some brickwork. Those dollies who got lucky are off laying their future families in the multi-storeyed nettles, and only the more debonair Honey Bees are mad enough to go out in the mid-day sun. Once in a while an Englishman and his dog passes by the bush, as it drapes over the fence and into the street.

But ridiculing the aesthetics of the buddleia bush and its vortex of sunshine activities is really unfair because this native of north-west China is an invaluable asset to garden insect life. It was discovered growing on shingle beds and scree by a French missionary, Père David, who sent seeds back to Europe and named the species after an English clergyman, Bishop Buddle.

Arriving at Kew in 1896, this colourful shrub soon found favour with Victorian gardeners, and its wind-borne seeds ensured its presence on any broken ground. Buddleia's thick lilac flower trunks are rich in nectar, and attract a great diversity of butterflies, moths, hoverflies, bees, flies and beetles. Very few of these visitors can find any more use for the plant though. Only a few moth larvae can eat the leaves, so like many non-native species it is ecologically inert.

What buddleia needs is a good strong bed of stinging nettles as a complementary food source. Here the larvae of butterflies such as Peacock, Red Admiral and Small Tortoiseshell frolic and feed in safety, relying on the fiercely barbed leaves to ward off rash-wary predators. However, the ferocity of nettle is not only directed at the hands of gardeners, blackberry pickers and a host of herbivores. It is one of the most aggressive and competitive plants in Britain, inflicting cruelty on other plants through some extraordinary adaptations.

That the nettle is an effective competitor on its favoured nitrogen-rich soils is undoubtable. Carefully peer into the canopy of one of those dark green, spreading beds of the species at the height of the summer. The soil below the stems will be almost naked, decorated with a few scraps of last year's detritus. No other plant can stand this rude barbarian. It is a light hog, which outcompetes other plants for this

Above: *This appears to be an ideally suited bush in terms of all day sunshine. In stronger breezes and wind most butterflies prefer a little more shelter, so you might try filling any shielded suntraps with this species to ensure maximum appeal.*

valuable resource, enabling rapid intake of nutrients under crowded conditions to produce lots of leaf material. The design of the leaves, their arrangement, shape, thickness, and the distribution of the light-hungry chlorophyll in the plant tissues enable it to maximize its use of light and grow, grow, grow! Everything else is left to decay in the shade.

Above: *What a combo! More colourful than you could shake a very colourful paint set at. Red Admiral (top) and Peacock (bottom) all dressed up for a summer's fling. A trifle gaudy, but firm family favourites, both species are on the wing throughout the milder months and hibernate as adults. With only a modicum of stealth you can pry into their privacy and watch their proboscis probing. Nice!*

PHOTOGRAPHY

BASIC PRINCIPLES

These days wildlife photography is extremely popular, with a great many professionals and amateurs taking advantage of a superb range of easy-to-use equipment – in fact there are few technically limited challenges left, now it's all down to the subject. And as a subject what could be a greater, richer and a more enigmatic and widely appealing resource? Not even the nude! So why is it that as a genre

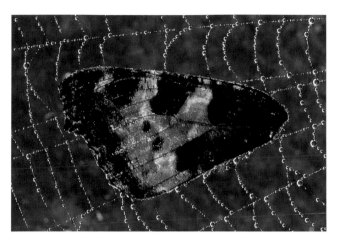

wildlife photography is still in the artistic doldrums? Why is it that the fine art establishment ignores its very finest practitioners as 'hicks who chase animals' while exhibiting and printing mediocre snaps of most other subjects?

I believe it's the legacy of the past, a past blighted by the embarrassing acclaim we bestowed upon those who merely captured their subject, irrespective of photographic, let alone artistic, quality. We all said 'wow' just because it was rare, shy, difficult, sharp or properly exposed, and frankly none of these matter an iota. What counts is that the subject has been uniquely interpreted and presented in an interesting or invigorating manner. That the photograph has communicated something to us, something personal, some idea we haven't had or seen or dreamt of. As you can tell this predicament irks me and many others. I've long been an advocate of taking a hard line on the mundane replication of reality and banishing those imperfect photographs which we enjoy just because the animal is doing something unusual. Dump it! 'If it's not art, don't even save it' was a maxim that I adhered to for years. My library is not extensive!

But I have become a little more tolerant. I don't quite like wallpaper yet, but I'm happier to accept that not everything has to be perfect, or say something or be 'high art'. Some things can just be nice, easy to live with, happy or curious. And they can be all these things and still be a very good photograph, maybe even a picture. But I still can't imagine why anyone would bother to pick up a camera and load it if they didn't at least start with

Left: Pattern can be useful in picture making. Here a small tortoiseshell's wing held in a spider's web incorporates its veins into the spangled structure to tell a story of fragility and predation.

the intention of taking a good photograph. So it's on this account that I implore you to aim high. You have a pair of eyes connected to a mind that has never been before nor ever will be again and everyone is capable of taking a great picture or two. Don't be lazy, look at a few fundamentals such as colour, texture, balance, composition, as well as photographic technique and integrate them into your ideas and photographs. Aim to take shots that you might want to hang on your wall, or better still that others might wish to hang on theirs. Be hard on your results, be ruthless, draconian. Prune and cut and discard until you're on the brink of having nothing left and then ask yourself again how your picture could be better.

Lastly, if you ever take a picture that you really think is perfect, throw all your equipment into the sea and give up! Actually, mail it to me because I haven't got there yet and hopefully never will. Perfection is personally unobtainable, reality is invariably horrible so achieving any satisfaction should take all eternity. Buy lots of film!

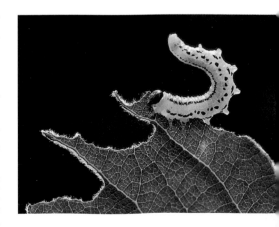

Above: Be alert to interesting patterns and motifs; here the repeated curved shape of a chewed leaf and the culprit make a little something out of virtually nothing.

YOUR GARDEN STUDIO

For the budding wildlife photographer the garden is the best studio available, and it doesn't matter how big your garden grows because our wildlife is all relatively small – no elephants, rhinos or herds of Wildebeest, and foxes, squirrels, frogs and insects can fit into the most conservative spaces, if not into a conservatory itself!

There are many benefits of working at home but privacy is probably top of the list. You see, if you decide to build a set or wish to leave your tripod out for an hour, it won't be interfered with, unlike anything you try to do in our over-populated countryside.

So you've designed a masterpiece and constructed your set. Now, because you are at home you can keep trying until you get it right. Time and privacy are great luxuries but there is also one unfortunate enemy of this cosy home practice, the dreaded handicap – familiarity. There is no doubt at all that at worst it breeds contempt, and at best laziness.

There is nothing so invigorating as the exotic, and if you take photographs and have travelled with your camera you'll know exactly what I mean. So here's the challenge: take the subject on your bird table, buddleia or back windowsill, and look again. Generate a new photographic excitement about those most accessible, convenient and

Left: House spider on blown lightbulbs. A curious set maybe, but the bubbles are better than a dusty garage floor. As usual, a little artistic licence goes a long way.

easy subjects which you have previously overlooked, and then come up with something that no one else has seen or photographed before.

Years ago, when it hadn't apparently been done, I took a photograph of a fox through the bottom of a dustbin. For some time afterwards acquaintances would remark that they had seen it in magazines or books to which it had never been sent. When I looked I found that other photographers had replicated my shot and some of their pictures were better. Good luck to them – it's the picture that counts!

Okay, you've researched the competition, you've readied the camera, it's time to take control. You've got to get to grips with the light, the colour, the texture, the composition and the position of the camera and its lens and your subject.

Let's consider a Robin on the bird table. Firstly, in front of the camera the bird table is not a bird table, it has become a photographic platform. I don't care whether Conran or Chippendale created your feeding station, neither I, nor most people, would wish to see it in the picture – we all like birds to look as if they are in the wild. And to fool us is easy, just nip down to the woods and pick up a nicely sculptured piece of moss and lichen-covered branch, preferably windblown, and G-clamp it to the table top. Only momentary confusion will grip Robbie Robin before he pitches on a far more picturesque perch. You don't have to go 'au natural' either – rusty pipes, car bonnets and a huge pile of empty but brilliantly coloured paint tins have all been at times attached to my bird tables to provide a more interesting backdrop than my neighbour's out of focus garage door. And remember, if the light is not right, you can always reposition everything into the shade or into the sunshine, and a new or novel background can be pinned to your fence, propped up against the pagoda or painted on the wall. After all, it's your garden!

Left: Through the dustbin – such a simple idea, such a success, even if I do say so myself. New angles are literally everywhere, they won't all work but they're worth a look.

CHANGING THE ANGLE

Of course you should immediately aim higher than a Robin on the bird table. Take advantage of whatever wildlife subjects you have, especially those which are least upset by your constructive changes. I once built a cemetery -- lots of hardboard, lightweight tombstones and withering wreaths dotted a friend's lawn to get a shot of a fox which took food from her patio. However, not all the visitors will be as forgiving as the Robin. There's no doubt that some of the more timid will be instantly put off if they see you anywhere unusual. You will normally find that your subjects are more wary than you'd imagined they might be. As a general rule, animals rely on familiarity for security; thus as long as you are where they expect you to be, they're happy. Move outside these areas, step off the path or outside the shed and suddenly everything becomes cautious. Nevertheless, urban subjects should be quicker to adapt and it's easier for you to persevere.

I know of only one comfortable, centrally heated hide complete with tea, coffee or beer, that normally has an assistant standing by and is free to use, without booking, 365 days a year – my house. Before you consider going out into the cold or wet exploit, the indoor opportunities. Ideally, shoot from where you normally sit or stand, from your armchair in front of the patio window or out of the kitchen window over the washing up. In this way you'll stand little or no chance of terrifying your thoroughly accustomed subjects. Obviously clean both sides of the glass and try to find a scratch-free section to line up with your lens. To minimize the risk of reflection keep the lens as close to the pane as possible, almost touching it is best. If you do need to use flash, get an extension lead to run out through the window to the gun which you've taped to a second tripod or stand and clad in a polythene bag to stop any rain getting in. This may take your subject a few days to get used to so flatten a couple of batteries flashing without film – by then all but the most timid visitors will be prepared to bask in a brief lightning strike.

If your lenses won't reach, or the bird table or set can't be moved close enough to a window then you have two choices; firstly you could fire the camera by remote, trigger cables can be bought for most cameras. Manually focus on

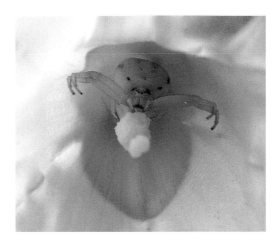

Left: *White and waiting, a crab spider poised to pounce in the tunnel of a bindweed bloom. By excluding any background I've simplified the picture and thrown all the focus onto the animal.*

the spot where the subject will be and lock the focus off. Using auto exposure you should be confident enough not to keep running back and forth to the camera to make adjustments. A motor drive or an auto-winder is essential, both fairly standard on today's SLRs. Use another polythene bag to protect the camera from Mr Moisture – secure it with a couple of elastic bands to stop it flapping in front of the lens. You can get perfect pictures using this approach but it's always nerve racking and will test the most confident practitioner. One word of caution; if Grey Squirrels are active in your garden be careful what you leave out unattended and unprotected. Irrespective of value, they will chew it and this will really upset you!

The second option is a case of moving outside yourself. Check the conservatory, greenhouse, garage, or outside toilet windows for prospective vantage points – if none are suitable build a hide out of anything. Remember it's your garden, so what it looks like is up to you; make it dry, comfortable and flap proof so that when the wind blows it doesn't startle your subject or expose you to it. Family camping tents, especially toilet tents, are easily 'cannibalized' or you can build more permanent structures from fencing panels, whatever; the choice is yours, and that of the family you have to live with. Remember they will have to barbecue, hang out the washing or play football around your structure.

Standing up straight or sitting down are among the most comfortable options, and if you have to spend hours waiting, comfort is essential. But this approach can in turn often mean that you end up looking down on your small ground-based subject, something which always appears unnatural and is therefore the mark of a lazy photographer. Get down to your subject's level; if you lie down, support the camera on a bean bag, and peer through the glass or over the pond, your perspective will make an immediate impact in a photograph. It increases the 'wildness' and reduces its domesticity.

INDEX

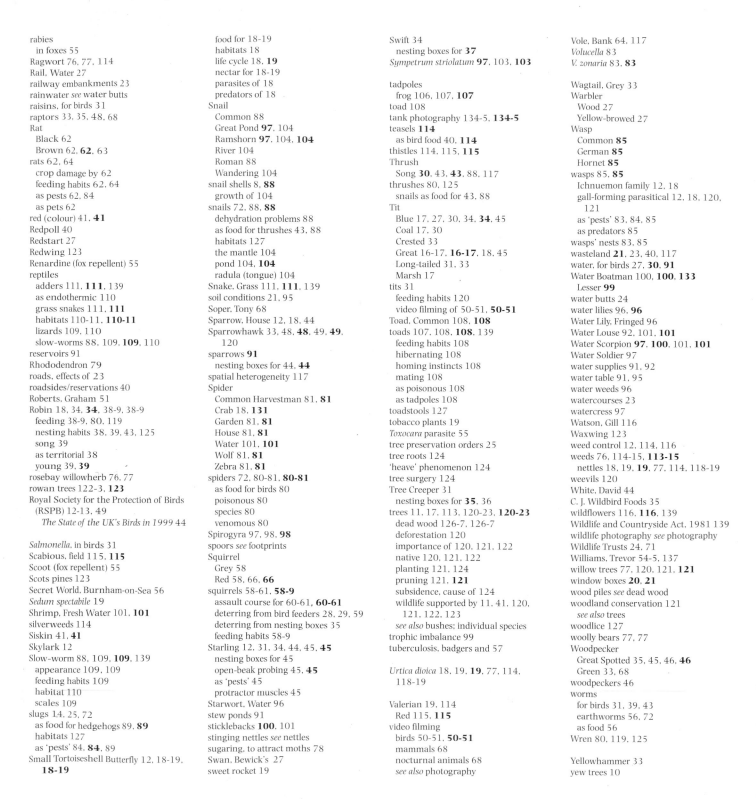

AUTHOR'S ACKNOWLEDGEMENTS

I would like to thank Chris Mead, David White and Chris Whittles for boosting the birdy bit, Tony Hutson, Graham Cornick, Pauline Kidner and Trevor Williams for helping to maximize the mammal potential, Nick Eden and Alexander Whish for taking the trouble to talk trees, David Cottridge for supplying most of the photographs, Jo Hemmings, Sylvia Sullivan and Mike Unwin for editorial energies, Barbara Levy for literal logistics, and Rita Packham and Joe McCubbin for taking the trouble to type all this.